TO THE BRINK

TO THE BRINK

Journal of a Student Pilot

JANUARY 12TH–NOVEMBER 5TH, 1975

DAVID C. NEWCOMB

Epigraph Books
Rhinebeck, New York

To the Brink: Journal of a Student Pilot, January 12th–November 5th, 1975 Copyright © 2024 by David C. Newcomb

Paperback ISBN 978-1-960090-97-3
Hardcover ISBN 978-1-960090-98-0
eBook ISBN 978-1-960090-99-7

Book design by Colin Rolfe

Epigraph Books
22 East Market Street, Suite 304
Rhinebeck, NY 12572
(845) 876-4861
epigraphpublishing.com

TO THE BRINK

I.

I undertook to learn how to fly in order to know what a pilot experiences. Flying had enchanted me from childhood, which for me encompassed the years following the Second World War. That was a time – the nineteen forties and fifties - when Hollywood and technology worked magic on the sensibilities of a boy.

From the second grade in grade school on, I was hooked on the romance and glamor of flying. Even later, at the age of thirty-three, at a time when the B-17 was a relic, I still wanted to fly one.

Instead, I settled for a Piper Cub, which, as any fool who's flown one knows, can scare a man to death. What follows is the story of the lessons I learned.

On January twelfth, 1975, I called a friend who had recently retired after a career in the FAA and who himself was a pilot. I asked him for advice about how to begin. He suggested that I start with ground school and that I call the board of education in Montgomery County, Maryland, to find out the curriculum for adult education. I made the call and was referred directly to the instructor of the course, Jim Heldenbrand. As it turned out, Jim was an engineer for the National Bureau of Standards and someone who considered teaching an avocation and aviation a hobby. He was teaching ground school to student pilots, private pilots seeking instrument ratings, and commercial pilots. On the phone Jim advised me there would be a formal meeting for purposes of registration at the Parklawn Junior High School (in Rockville, Maryland) on January twenty-first.

Evenings at Parklawn abounded with activities. There were courses taught in a number of subjects, including a classroom filled to capacity with women studying automobile repairs. In our classroom for aviation ground school, we sat at desks appropriate for children but too small for adults. Six students, all men, and Jim came for the registration, and Jim informed us that the class would ultimately number twenty-one students. He planned to combine the commercial ground school class with the class for private pilots. We six tonight were in the latter group.

Regarding my classmates, I made three observations. A man in the back of the room caught my attention first. He was rough-hewn, heavy-set, and spoke in tones louder than the teacher's. He had a side-kick, and the two of them had the back of the room to themselves. Nearer to the front, another man caught my attention by extolling the virtues of the Maryland Civil Air Patrol. He tried selling us on the idea of joining, but oversold his point and included the drawbacks – work parties and duty weekends – along with the virtues – reduced rates and a choice of planes and instructors. Regarding Jim, I could see that he was middle aged and trim, and in time I came also to see that he was cordial, conscientious, and meticulous in class.

The business of this first class was brief. We ordered books and paid for them. The fee for tuition and materials totaled one hundred fifteen dollars. Jim announced we would have eighty hours of class time in total, and would meet on Mondays and Thursday, from seven-thirty p.m. until ten, beginning February tenth and lasting into June. The format for the course would include discussions and reviews of chapters in class, tests on each of twelve chapters from the text, slides with narration supplied by the Sanderson Company of Denver, whose texts, workbooks, and study guides we would use. Jim warned us that for every hour we spent in class we would spend two hours at home on our own. On that prediction, if on no other, Jim was wrong. I spent closer to four.

* * *

I called my friend and told him I had enrolled. I asked if he would help me find a flight instructor. He said he would be pleased to try.

A few days later he called back. He said he had talked to a friend of his, who recommended someone he had heard about who liked to fly and was qualified to teach. Such things are ever indirect. To find an instructor is anything but cut-and-dried. It happens more likely by happenstance, for it involves so many active choices on the part of all concerned. The instructor requires an airplane to be rented, which involves a fixed base operator who rents the airplane. Then, there is the schedule for the instructor, who may or may not be available when the student is, the vagaries of the weather, the schedule for the airplane, the crowded competition for weekends, the choice of airports, and the schedule, convenience, whim, or ignorance of the student, who wants the best but can't tell what that is.

So, I took my available lead and called this man, Weamsley, whom my friend's friend had recommended. Although my call went to him out of the blue, Weamsley talked to me as if he had known me for a lifetime. Gloria washed the dishes while Weamsley talked to me. She cooked the dinner while Weamsley talked. I grunted now and then to interject some sound from my end. Gloria held dinner and read the *Washington Post*, but we weren't finished yet. She started the *downs* of the *Post's* crossword puzzle, when Weamsley finally said good-night to me. "Yes?" Gloria asked.

"You got me," I replied. Weamsley had, more or less, accepted me as his student. We were to begin later, an indefinite time. The signal to begin would come from him; he would call me. I must stand fast. Weamsley was almost ready to get his flight instructor's license. He would have it before this spring. Certainly before spring, since he was the manager of a Little League team.

* * *

To be perfectly honest, February is almost as slow as January.

MONDAY, FEBRUARY 10TH.

Ground school began. Competition began, even before the class. I was not the first there, though I was early. A dozen men had arrived ahead of me and they were conspicuous, even at a distance, at the end of the hall where six of them sat on a wide, low window ledge and the other six stood before them. Those dozen men stopped their talk to look at me when I arrived. Could it be that I looked as unfriendly to them as they did to me? Let's find out. I say hello. No one answers. I win the toss. I think I'll receive.

Competition for prestige here was based on talk, though the order of ranking was suggested by the way we stood or sat. Those who sat seemed to have more, and he who sat in the middle of the window ledge was none other than the bully, flanked by his sidekick. The bully held court. He dominated the conversation, all of whose references were to airplanes and to flying skills. It was, it seemed, an object lesson in mystification; facility with jargon implied a big stick. I felt distinctly out of this and took my place on the outskirts of the group. I stood, as others out here did, with my profile to the window ledge; in my case to show how tenuous was the bond that kept me here. As more people came, however, the center of the group no longer contained the periphery and yielded to local conversations. It became apparent that people lowest in the order of things were friendliest; the people on the outskirts of the group were the ones who said hello.

Jim arrived, and all this nonsense stopped. He said hello, and everyone replied. We were the ducklings and he was the hen (sic). Cluck, cluck, cluck, and off we went to room C-3. But, once we reached our classroom, the same pretensions that governed our rankings in the hall applied to our seating arrangements. Since I could lay claim to no competence in flying, I expressed my ambition by choosing the first seat in the second row from the right, which was the nearest seat to the teacher's desk.

For several moments Jim resumed the details of registration and ordering texts. The texts had not yet come. I continued my observations of the group. Not only had we no women, we were exclusive in other ways too. We had no one very young; only five of twenty-one of us appeared to be under thirty. We were middle class. Talk tells. I could confirm this later: general aviation does not allow the poor. There may have been among us someone rich, a condition easier to hide. But middle class ends up a frame of mind. Once we were settled, we retained our strained relations from outside. The man I was characterizing as a bully, and his buddy, chose the two seats farthest from Jim, all the way back in the two left rows. Ahead of them was a younger man, a braggadocio, whose exploits fell from his tongue as fast as his friends could applaud. In the same left row, ahead of him, was the enthusiast for the Civil Air Patrol. And at the head of the row sat a brooder who seemed bound up in his nerves. He tossed a paper wad at the basket and missed. I had the sense that he hated to fetch it from the floor, but he knew he'd been observed. To his right sat a very studious fellow seeming buried in arcane reading material. He and I were the only two who sported beards. And to my right sat the first of our several engineers. His row was engineers' row, right on back to the end, Joe, who was a dentist. My row was a mish-mash; I wrote. The guy behind me sold insurance. The guy at the end drove a bus.

The first order of business that Jim addressed to the group concerned an introduction. Since we were going to be there for a long time, through a long haul, Jim wanted us to introduce ourselves, man by man, around the room. I found of a sudden the room lacked air to breath. I was clearly nervous. We started down the right row, allowing me to compute how many people would speak before my turn came up. The first man was a communications engineer. The second man had served as a B-24 pilot during World War II. He, too, was an engineer but had been out of touch with aviation since the war. Remo Ciccone was third. He was a bright young man, very affable, and a pilot who was working toward his commercial license. Joe Earle was last in line, which put me next. Joe was a dentist, and a private pilot who co-owned a plane. He flew for his own recreation and enrolled in the commercial course simply to add to his knowledge. I turned front, my doodling done.

"I am David Newcomb," I began. "I come from Cincinnati." As if that weren't enough, I added, "I'm a writer. For the past three years I have been doing research on bomber crews who flew for the Eighth Air Force during World War II. It occurred to me, finally, that I was missing an experience at the center. I had to learn to fly a plane if I was going to write the piece." With that, I stopped. I truly had my audience. No pedestrian reasoning for me. No idle curiosity brought me here. I came to the plate to swing my bat.

Somebody in the back piped up. "What'd he say? All we heard was 'Cincinnati.'

On the second time through, for Jim asked if I would repeat my tale in a louder voice, I repeated it verbatim, which astonished me and won the approval of the insurance salesman who sat behind me in the row. In fact, so solidly had I won his admiration that he distracted me as I spoke by nodding his head as I went along. It was as if my spiel had been addressed to him, and I think, on looking back, perhaps it was.

The introductions went along merrily after that, for no one holds my interest the way I hold my own. Henry was the salesman. Bob Dubin, behind Henry, owns an airplane but didn't have his license yet. Behind Dubin sat Posie Preston; he had a license to fly and had entered the commercial course. In the seat to my left, the studious person was Malcolm Sanders, "Sandy," who was an oceanographer with the Naval Oceanographic Research Station at Suitland, Maryland. He was unique in the class because he alone had no intentions of learning to fly. He had, as he said, several friends who were involved in building experimental airplanes, and he wanted to learn something of their tasks. Behind Sandy sat two graduate students in engineering.

Then we came to Bill Miller, the man I have been labelling a bully. Bill Miller was an old coot, you see, tough as nails. But the truth of the matter is that he really was tough as nails. He had been hanging in for thirty years, waiting his chance, waiting to do what he had wanted to do since the forties: get a pilot's license. Bill was a foreman for the Potomac Electric Power Company. He worked out of doors, with a line crew. In World War II he was a crew chief with the Army Air Forces. That is where his life has been: running a gang and at work with his hands. He did not feel abashed in a room of engineers; they did not scuttle him. They scuttled me. Bill came on all gruff, feigned rudeness, practiced the voice of experience because he had that voice. If I felt I had no place in that room, as a humanist, Bill felt entirely in place there, as a human being.

Jim had something to say on that as well. He told Bill he felt envious of him and he told him why. Because Bill was his own man; to that extent, free. Those of us who shoved papers back and forth, pushed words, who looked on at the world through a window, must make our peace with that. Once Jim said it, I felt obliged to reconsider Jim (and to think about my own role there). There was more to Jim than the book and the rules. I believe Jim made the remark in order to embrace a class.

The introductions resumed on the far left row. A chocolate malt never sounded so good in my life. The man who struck me as bound-up appeared to identify himself as same. He came to aviation at the end of a list of hobbies all of which are achievement-oriented and competitive and included sports car racing and karate. He worked with the National Wildlife Federation, serving the post of acting director. Behind him, Alan Ferreira was the advocate for the C.A.P. Alan worked for the National Institute of Health as a virologist. Teddy Odder was the young man of exploits. At the age of twenty-three he already owned his own business; he enrolled here for a commercial pilot's license. At the end of the row sat Ron Ament, who had been Bill Miller's partner in their chats. Ron had far more than friendship in common with Bill, however, for he too served in the Air Force as a crew chief. But Ron had a license and owned his own plane. At the end of Ron's introduction, Jim chimed in, "And I know you are very proud of your Cherokee, Ron," by which Jim meant

Ron's Piper airplane, his Cherokee One-forty. And by which I understood him to imply that those who own their own are proud. Must be. And those who have to rent are not. Man and his horse. Again. The Western myth had been seized upon for Twentieth Century usage now. Technology made the figure even older than a horse: Man with Wings.

*　*　*

Intermission combined some sample rituals for us. We went to the faculty lounge to drink our Cokes, and we went in the same pairings, or alone, or in the same small groups we had established in the hall before the class. Inside the lounge, we segregated according to who smoked. Typically, the most sociable exchange of the break occurred when somebody asked change for a dollar to buy himself a Coke. Even the ashtray had to be passed back and forth at the table, so little sharing took place tonight. Eventually, when we would soften up, in a week or so, we would go so far as to bum a cigarette or offer a light. Eventually, beyond that, we would go so far as to do what students do on break the school world over; we would bitch about the prof. But for tonight the introductions had failed to soften us at all. Men among themselves might as well arm wrestle and be done with it.

When a messenger sent by Jim appeared at the door to tell us we were due back again, we set out from the lounge as routinely as migratory birds. We resumed our patterns down the long hall back. Shop talk meant success tonight. No one wanted to give up anything; everything was defensible. We would have to wait. Group behavior does not make a class.

In the room again we spent the remainder of the time being shown slides, while Jim overrode the film's narrator to make comments or ask questions of his own. He was trying, by every trick he knew, as a teacher who had been through it all before, to gather us. It brought one result, at least. By the end of the class we were commonly tired.

It was ten thirty when we departed. Hardly a shred of conversation or a "good night" distinguished anyone from anyone as we rifled down the hall. The only sounds I heard clearly came from jacket zippers zipping up.

En route to home I stopped and got my malt. Jim had said in passing that before the course was over, quite a few of us would drop out. He had that point of view.

THURSDAY, FEBRUARY 13TH.

When Jim came, he lugged a dolly. On the dolly sat the boxes with our books. The books seemed to act as pacifiers. They brought a hush over the class. As each of us received our own text, we leafed through the pages. I matched the chapter heads against the dates in the course schedule set aside for tests. I wanted to see how much time separated each test, so I could match that notion of time with what I saw as the body of each chapter in the text. Such looking ahead served only to create the feeling of being overwhelmed. Apparently other people had done the same. I heard some groans from around the room. I had already heard some gripes about the difficulties of coming home from work, gobbling dinner, and then rushing off to spend the balance of the evening in ground school. The text appeared formidable. I was glad we had six months.

A humanist adapts. I recognized that to be the point of an education in the liberal arts, though it was not taught as such when I attended school. We began a discussion of aerodynamics. Jim asked the questions. People raised their hands to answer. Sometimes the group as a whole joined in the response. If anything stands out in a unison response, it is a wrong note in a chorus of right ones. On one question, Jim asked whether or not lift would be in a state of equilibrium with gravity if an airplane were climbing at a constant rate of climb. The whole room seemed to chime in unison: Yes it would. Except for the two clunkers, Bill Miller's and mine. No it wouldn't, we said. Bill looked at me. And I looked at him. It seemed we just made friends.

11

The class ended at ten minutes to eleven, clearly too late. My eyes had become salty from the forced-air ventilation in the room. When Jim said good night, he might as well have rallied the Grand Prix. It was "Drivers, to your cars."

* * *

It was at home that I came into my own. I have a need to know and I met it best on my own terms, home, alone. It is not necessary to know how the design of an airplane produces its effects in flight. It is necessary only to know how the airplane responds. Ground school serves the practical purpose of giving knowledge that will be useful in flight. Useful is the key word. Usable. Full of use. To go beyond that is academic unless you intend to build airplanes, or repair them. Even to repair them, it is not necessary to know the ends and the means to the ends of the features that produce lift and stabilize an airplane as it flies. There are pilots who fly beautifully knowing only behavior. And there are mechanics who work by instinct, memory and the book. Nor is it possible in flying to think logically about the act of flight while doing the act. One precedes the other, sometimes by a gap of months. Yet I have a need to know. I seem unable to proceed for purely practical purposes. For me, it is no wonder that the biological class, AVES (birds), reached an evolutionary dead-end. No motion is more subtle than bird's flight.

MONDAY, FEBRUARY 17TH.

No class. Holiday.

THURSDAY, FEBRUARY 20TH.

We continued our sessions on aerodynamics. During intermission I learned from Bill Miller that he got up every day at five forty-five to go to work. Whether he said it to invoke my sympathy or not, he had it, for ground school made his day too long. On the way back to class

I had a chance to speak with George Nutwell, a bright-eyed, somewhat foxy graduate student in engineering. George asked, in a mischievous, just slightly skeptical way, what it was like to be a writer. I took a good look at George. He has quick, sharp eyes, a pointy nose. He is thin, he wears turtlenecks, and his mouth is forever playing at a smile. I told him the biggest problem was how to cast characters to suit a given work. He bought it. At least he went away. Of course, the biggest problem really is: how to put a word where there is space.

Our braggadocio shot off his mouth as we settled in our seats for the second half of class. He told us of a flight he just made in a twin engine airplane, which he called a "really sweet bird." He said that during the flight the battery went dead and the airplane lost all of its electrical system. Obviously, he made it back. Near the end of the class I heard a new phrase, which came from Jim, and which stuck in my mind: "To grease it on." A thought passed through my mind, what Hamlet once said: "Ay, there's the rub."

Monday, February 24th

We entered the area of study called weight and balance, its theory and computation. Nutwell asked if I had an instructor yet and had I started to fly. He was flying at Montgomery County Air Park, near the town of Gaithersburg, and his lessons were well under way. I told him I'd had a cold lately but I'd get started soon. At intermission I sat with Bill Miller.

Jim related to us an anecdote about some people who were going to fly to upstate New York during the winter and have a ski party week-end. There were two couples. They were flying a four-seat. By the time everybody boarded and the ski equipment and gear were stowed in back, the pilot suspected the plane might be overweight. He did a rough calculation of the passengers' weight and that of the gear. The airplane was in fact overweight by fifty pounds. He remedied the situation while on the ground by burning off fifty pounds of fuel. In an airplane that size the engine burns several gallons an hour, and since fuel weighs six pounds per gallon it did not take long before the plane was down to its maximum gross weight. The pilot neglected, however, to check how the weight was distributed. The plane was tail heavy. There was too much weight behind the center of gravity, which caused the center of gravity to be located farther aft than was normal or permissible for stability. Jim never mentioned how the story ended.

THURSDAY, FEBRUARY 27TH

Jim announced the test which would come Monday. There was a general grumbling and mumbling among us, though I felt each of us was relieved. Whether we were prepared or ever would be was immaterial, for, apart from every other value, a test serves one decided purpose. It puts an end to effort.

I took stock by the end of the class. I was on speaking terms now with half the students. As we departed from the building. I could hear about a dozen different comments concerning what lay ahead. It was the comeuppance. It was the penance for delay, the price of laziness, the fault of circumstances, the promise of catastrophe. We were beginning to sound like a group of human beings.

MONDAY, MARCH 3RD.

Tonight was it and we were a-buzz. I never heard so many rationales or so much ardor in their expression. One man complained he couldn't crack a book until Sunday night. Another had to go out of town and didn't get back until two hours ago. Another's child was sick with flu. It sounded like the last Reckoning. Six of us were absent.

Jim gave us two exams, each with twenty-five multiple-choice questions, and we began at twenty minutes to eight. The first exam covered aerodynamics, the components of an airplane, and the ways in which an airplane performs when it flies. The second exam covered the theory of weight and balance, with computations pertinent to problems of that sort. For about two hours the room filled with sounds of erasers scrubbing worksheets, with sounds of ticks coming out of calculators, with moans, with muffled moans, with yawns, an occasional "cripes," or worse, and with the impacts of pencil points on pads.

At the end of the test, we retired to the lounge for a break. A bit of magic had transformed us by that test. We had a common enemy now: it was the Sanderson Company. In the lounge we were together, in the psychological way of the word. We had become bonded. Now we were a class.

Nutwell asked me questions, to dig out what I knew. What did I know? I thought I knew it all. I told him I didn't know. Somebody wanted to know: what did you get for an answer to that question.... Which one? Number thirteen, about Angle of Attack? Can't remember. Oh yes. It was.... So it went, for ten minutes, with wails of chagrin from those who just then realized they had missed one they thought they knew. Arguments erupted, on a friendly line of fire. Everyone agreed the test posed trick questions, that it was poorly devised and ambiguous in its wording. We all wondered whether Jim would take sides with the Sanderson people; then we would blame him, too.

For the remainder of class time we graded papers. Jim went through the questions one-by-one. We booed and hooted and hollered, and the reckoning arrived. We gave in our scores. On giving scores, everyone wanted to know what everyone else got, and there was a considerable hubbub in finding out. And that was the end of solidarity, for the test made us a class by giving us a common ordeal, and the grading of the test classified us, according to our scores.

* * *

The FAA requires private pilots to pass a physical examination every two years, and student pilots must pass it before they are allowed to fly solo. I began to perceive that the life of a student pilot was a series of bottlenecks. The student must get through each bottleneck before he or she can arrive at the next one. During my physical, the physician found that I had a heart murmur, and the FAA required that I be referred to a cardiologist for further examination.

THURSDAY, MARCH 6TH.

No class. Jim was out of town.

MONDAY, MARCH 10TH.

Those who failed to take the tests a week ago and those who failed either of the two tests themselves began to make arrangements with Jim for special make-up sessions and tutoring, at additional expense. We had to pass each of the twelve tests to pass the course. This was part of what I meant by bottlenecks.

We began studying the systems of an airplane. I felt reasonably secure in the work now. On the other hand, I felt less than secure about my motives in the class. Perhaps my original ardor to fly had come a cropper. In any case, I seemed to be clinging to competence in school as a surrogate for the nerve I lacked to try my hand at flight.

The systems of an airplane relate the pilot to the conditions of flight, or to the progress of the flight at a particular juncture, or to the behavior of the airplane itself. The systems extend the pilot. For that, we speak in terms whereby the pilot is the one who executes the moves rather than the airplane, and the pilot is the one who owns the parts of the airplane. "I made the turn." "I turned." "I turned final and slipped." "My wings." "My prop." "My rudder." The instruments provide the pilot with extensions of the senses. "Well, my oil temperature was on the rise and I lost some R.P.M.'s." The flight controls extend the pilot's motor nerves. "I dropped the flaps and pushed my nose down." A flight instructor will use those terms objectively, often in accusatory tones. "You're letting your airspeed get too fast. You're letting your nose down too far. You're using your rudder too much." All those things are properties of the pilot, even the student pilot. You're the pilot. It's your airspeed, your altitude, your attitude; your wings that are not level with the earth. Learning to fly includes learning to disregard the translation from you, the pilot, to it, the airplane. The two of you are simply you.

There are several systems in an airplane; the engine alone makes use of several. It has a fuel system, ignition system, cooling system and exhaust system, plus it provides the power to drive the charging system, which includes an alternator, regulator and battery, and is, in turn, the source of power for the electrical system. There are the flight controls and trim, and they are a system. And there are the instruments, which are divided into subsystems themselves. There are engine-monitoring instruments; gyroscopic instruments, which pertain to the attitude of the airplane and stability; pilot-static instruments, which include the altimeter and the airspeed indicator; and navigational instruments, which relate to the use of radio.

The engine of an airplane differs from that of an automobile in four important respects. For one, it is a lighter engine; its block is cast in aluminum. For another, it is air cooled, and so simpler. Further, an airplane engine derives its spark, its ignition, from magnetos, and those work independently of the electrical system. Should there be a fuse blown, a battery failure, an alternator malfunction or a short circuit, should the entire electrical system go out, the engine still runs. Finally, the ignition system is doubled. There are two sets of spark plugs, two plugs in each cylinder, and each set of plugs is powered by a separate magneto. Should one magneto or one of its spark plugs fail, the other backs it up. An airplane engine represents generalized design simplicity because it needs to respond to changes in environment that are sometimes rapid and sometimes extreme. Demands put upon it vary widely. Designers, wittingly or no, have harked back to the lessons of natural law for the model: the creature that is simple, adapts. The automobile engine, by contrast, has become complex and specialized. It is a fitting irony that the gasoline it burns was once the flesh of dinosaurs.

* * *

Wednesday I saw a cardiologist. She forwarded the results of her examination to the Airmen's Certification Branch of the FAA, located in Oklahoma City. It seems that at birth a tricuspid valve was formed with two cusps instead of three. We live by gauges in everything we do.

Wednesday evening, I made an application to the FCC for a Restricted Radiotelephone Operator Permit. After that, uncertainty got the best of me and I screwed up my nerve to call Weamsley, the man who was to be my flight instructor, or so we had agreed. While I was placing the call Gloria sat opposite me on the sofa and worked the crossword puzzle from the _Post_. She pretended not to overhear.

Weamsley's wife answered the phone. She told me he was in the other room talking to friends and asked me was it important. I told her who I was and why I was calling. I repeated the whole thing Weamsley and I went through six weeks ago; how he had said he was about to get his instructor's certificate and how he'd like to take me as his student, but that I was to wait and he would get in touch with me. She went to get him. He came to the phone. He didn't know who I was. I told him. He didn't really remember talking to me. I asked him if he got his instructor's certificate yet. He told me he had no plans to get his instructor's certificate; he was coaching Little League that Spring.

When I hung up the phone, I looked at Gloria. At length, she looked up at me. "He flunked his test," she said.

THURSDAY, MARCH 13TH.

I avoided Nutwell and sought out the company of Bill Miller. I told Bill about my problem with the cardiologist's report and asked him how the FAA would rule on that. He told me not to worry, that he passed his medical and he's already had three heart attacks.

At the end of class time I stayed after to ask Jim a question concerning carburetors and carburetor heat, a subject we had been discussing. Jim was amenable. I said, "If you pull the carburetor heat on, the air in the throat of the carburetor becomes warmer, therefore less dense."

"That's right," he said and slipped into his overcoat.

"Okay," I said, "If it's less dense, that changes the mixture. It makes the mixture too rich. So you should lean the mixture, right?"

"Well, technically you're right," Jim said.

"Okay, so why don't pilots do it?"

He gathered his materials. He seemed to consider it. He made ready to go. "When do you pull the carburetor heat on?" he asked. "As a rule."

I stared at him.

He took a few steps and stopped. "When?" he asked.

I didn't have anything to say.

"How much flying are you doing?" he asked, just as distantly and coolly as he could. "How many hours do you have?"

"I haven't started yet," I said. "The guy who was going to instruct me flunked his test."

"Oh," said Jim.

"I thought it would be better to finish ground school first and then fly."

"Well it isn't," he said flatly.

"'Well, wouldn't it be better?" I asked. "Wouldn't that make learning to fly that much easier, if I already know the material before I started?"

"No it wouldn't," Jim said, and coolly bid me good-night.

Outside, there was a fine, cold drizzle coming down. I headed for the car. I saw Bill Miller and Alan Ferreira, the enthusiast for the C.A.P., standing in the parking lot, in the drizzle, like mindless ducks. I joined the conversation. Bill bummed a cigarette from me. I told them of my quandary. Both were sympathetic. Alan invited me to join the Civil Air Patrol. He told me where the next meeting would be and what time. Bill told me he'd been flying out at Davis Airport. I asked him where that was. He said it was near Montgomery County Air Park. He told me he only paid eleven dollars an hour to rent a Piper Cub. He seemed abashed to talk about the Piper Cub. Since I didn't know one airplane from another, I asked him why. "Well, they're old airplanes," he said. "They're puddle jumpers. They're from World War II, or before." Alan told me that the Civil Air Patrol had several new planes, a variety from which to choose. Their rates were cheap, too, but you had to join the organization first. Bill said that at Davis they had other airplanes to rent, though they cost more than the Cub. He said the Cub was a forgiving ship, forgiving of pilots in error. Alan said Montgomery County had a longer runway and was a better equipped airfield. Bill said that if you can learn to land at Davis Airport, then you can land anywhere. Alan laughed. It seemed he conceded the point to Bill. "Come with me sometime," said Bill.

"Let me think on it," I said.

SATURDAY, MARCH 15TH.

We held a make-up class to account for the day Jim was out of town, and this class marked our regularly scheduled test covering the systems of an airplane. Other than that, the day dawned breezily and promised to be bright, a specimen of middle March.

I had come to the conclusion that Jim was right, that ground school could not be that interesting on its own, that what a pilot needed was information fast. The chapter on systems had opened me to the full inference of my conclusion. There was no end to what you can know about an airplane's systems; you could take each application and work backwards to the principle that founded it, and keep on doing that in a chain of refinements, discoveries, investigations that begins somewhere around Archimedes, or perhaps before, to the discoverer of the concept of pi. The figure of an airplane in flight seems to compose most of the discoveries of the laws of nature that have become the basis of Western scientific thought. It is possible to examine an airplane and derive a Who's Who of the history of ideas, Archimedes through Max Planck.

We took our test. At the end of our test we were educated men. Outside again, I found Bill Miller. "Rough," said Bill. "Sneaky," he said.

"When are you going flying again?" I asked.

"Tomorrow, if the weather's nice," he said.

"Mind if I go with you?"

"Meet me in front of Bernstein's bakery at the Aspen Hills Shopping Center," he said.

"What time?" I asked.

"At nine o'clock," he said.

SUNDAY, MARCH 16TH.

The morning was blustery fair. Bernstein's bakery was open before I arrived. I arrived before Bill. People were already in line inside the bakery, and a ventilator fan above the front door sent out an aroma of the morning's goods. Bill came and made a bee-line for the entrance. "Come on, come on," he said, so much the gruffer for the early hour. I followed him inside and he treated me to a selection of rolls and coffee. We ate in his car. He told me he prefers to start his days that way, that he had discovered all the bakeries in the county. Like so many men who were young a generation ago, Bill was self-reliant and, in equal parts, generous.

We drove out through the countryside, and the suburbs shed to farms. Sloped, rolling, knoll and hillock country appeared; the vistas no longer blocked by the yard-to-yard development of houses. And the progress of Spring was visible in the bright patches of very green grass that grew beside the drainage ditch along the road. We passed through the town of Laytonsville, on the road to the airport. It was an old town and a small one, whose commerce seemed limited to an antique shop, a general store, two service stations and an outlet for recapped tires. The houses are alternately white frame and tan stone, both types with steep rooves and chimneys front and rear, a style from early in this century or late in the last. Not far behind the houses cattle grazed. Horses stood by the fence along the road. I saw some signs, which advertised fresh eggs, and noted the headstones, carved of lime, had weathered into hues of green in the little graveyard behind the Methodist church.

I had the pleasure of reading Bill's log books, which he brought along. And as I read, he spoke of his family. He has three sons, now

grown, and two of them had entered college. All three of the sons
still lived at home, which was the precipitating factor in his own deci-
sion to enroll in ground school: it couldn't make things worse. I saw
that Bill was on his fourth log book. I also saw that the first entry in
the first log book dated from the Spring of 1944. His children had
not been born, and he was flying Piper Cubs.

A yellow airplane came into view. It flew across the road ahead
of us, from right to left, very low, and disappeared from view behind
a stand of hardwood trees. "There's your Piper Cub," said Bill. The
instant he said that I got a surge of adrenalin inside my belly. When
we passed the stand of trees, I saw the airport out to the left, and the
Cub, now landed, had begun to taxi back.

We turned off from the Laytonsville Road onto Hawkins Creamery
Road and turned again, shortly, into a driveway where the mailbox
was marked, "Davis Airport. W. H. Paille, Fixed Base Operator."

The airport had not changed substantially since it was founded, by
a man named Davis, some thirty years previously. It was a one-run-
way, rustic, country airport. There was a quonset-style hangar with
a yellow roof. An office adjoined it. The drive in was gravel over dirt
and the parking lot the same. Farm fences barely set the airport off
from the fields around it, and blackberry bushes grew by the fence
along the parking lot. Several other cars were here ahead of us. The
airplane that landed had taken off again, but another Piper Cub,
again all yellow, sat facing us, its nose to the nose of Bill's car. As
we parked, I marveled at that airplane, but I marveled at the runway
behind it, too, and at the whole airport for that, for I had never been
to a small airport before. The runway seemed no wider to me than a
driveway - a double driveway - and although it was long for a driveway, at two thousand two hundred feet, it was short for a runway.
Among the first things noticeable about that runway were its cants
and slopes and blacktopped humps and little bumps. In time, I would
become intimate with those.

The runway lay essentially east-west. Its bearings, numbered at
each end, "26" and "8", in numbers that were large and clearly visible from the air, stood for magnetic directions, 260 and 80 degrees,

reciprocally, from magnetic north. It amused me to see the textbook coming true. Across the runway, on the south side of the airport, I saw that large stand of hardwood trees I had seen from the road. I would become friends with those trees, or familiar with effects they create, at least when the winds are southwesterly and we were landing west on runway 26; they cause turbulence, eddies and downdrafts. In front of the trees stood the pole with the bright orange wind sock, partially inflated and standing out from the vertical mast. The winds today were gusting from the northwest. Runway 26 was active. Alongside the sock was the wind T, turned to indicate the active runway. The gusts of wind rocked the wings of the Cub, even tied. Beyond the Cub, a long row of airplanes sat parked, their noses to the fence and tails to the runway. Across the runway at the other end of the airport sat a score of airplanes, also parked in rows, their tails to me.

Bill took me into the office. He introduced me to Bill Paille (rhymes with daily), who proceeded to eye me up and down, perhaps as I did him. No one else was there, though we found out first thing that the airplanes and the instructors were all booked for the day. Frankly, I was relieved. Ever since we arrived at this place, my heart had been halfway in my throat. Bill Miller mentioned that I was trying to get started as a student. Bill Paille told me that I had come to the right place. "If you're serious, we can take you right on through," he said. He noticed me looking at the rental rates posted on the front of the glass counter, and added that I wouldn't find any place much cheaper than here. I saw the Cubs cost eleven dollars an hour, the Aeronca Champ, fourteen, the Piper Colt and Cessna 150, sixteen dollars each. I learned that the instruction costs eight dollars an hour and that I would make my own arrangements with an instructor. There were several flight instructors who associated with Laytonvsille Flying Service, the name of the organization Bill Paille operated.

I took it from the conversation that Bill Paille was particularly fond of the Cubs. He bought them beaten up and restored them to new, a meticulous, laborious process which often took a year. He was also a licensed airframe and engine mechanic and did repairs and inspections for most of the aircraft owners whose planes I saw parked outside. As Bill Miller would tell me later, Bill Paille held nearly every certificate and rating in the book. He was an interesting man. He looked interesting, full of lore, cagey. He had a shock of white hair and a weather beaten face, and he looked perfectly appropriate in an engineer's cap and coveralls. What did not fit the context, of the place, not the man, was his accent, which rang a bell immediately: Maine. Paille was down-East. His family was Canadian; his name corrupted by environment. He walked with the help of a cane. I jumped to the conclusion that he had suffered injuries in an accident. But that was not the case, though he had flown thousands and thousands of hours (he himself had lost count). He grew up in the era of barnstorming, and first flew as a young boy. It helped to date the experience when he recalled that the way they used to stop an airplane after it had landed was to reach out of the cockpit with gloved hands and grab the tires. During World War II he served as a ferry pilot for the Army Air Forces, and managed in the course of things to fly about every airplane this nation ever built. His appearance belied his actual age. He did not look sixty, when in fact he was sixty-eight. In the last few years, illness had forced him to give up active flying.

The Cubs were Paille's pride and joy. His face lit up when he spoke of them. Davis was one of the few airports where a student could learn in one of the airplanes that served a generation of pilots as a primary trainer. It is a tail-wheel airplane, and Paille told you that if you could learn to fly it then you had learned to fly. The alternative, the Cessna 150, had become the new standard trainer for a new generation of pilots. It is a tri-cycle geared (with nose wheel instead of tail wheel) airplane. It behaves, particularly in landing, altogether differently from the Cub. "Anyone can fly it," said Paille, with some traces of contempt ringing from his voice. "It's easy." Then he paused. "Try the Cub."

The conversation switched to how many hours it took to get a license now. "No body can do it in forty hours now," said Bill Miller.

"Not since they've added all those new requirements," agreed Paille. "Not many can do it in fifty, I would say."

Like Thomas Hardy's constable, I nodded knowingly, knowing nothing. I assumed I was a natural, of course. Whatever was minimum, I would make that. I had no idea what the new requirements were, or for that matter what the old ones had been before they were changed.

I liked Bill Paille's office. It was old, cluttered, functional. Things seemed in their place. His desk was an old pigeon-hole model, dark wood in need of a dusting. Boxes of airplane parts and gadgets lined the glass case behind his desk. A two-way radio sat on top of the filing cabinet. There was a planning table, for pilots to use during pre-flight reviews. And the office had four chairs, no two of a kind. There was an old, red clunker of a Coke machine that required you drop in a nickel and turn a crank. That caught my fancy most of all, though the machine was out of order, to say nothing of time, and was opposed by a new machine that stood on the other side of the office, cost more and required you to push a button. There were magazines stacked on the table; all of them pilots' magazines. There was a list of telephone numbers to flight service stations in the area, and a whole wall of the office was taken up by a planning chart which represented the eastern half of the United States. I saw a pin stuck in the chart to mark Davis Airport. On another wall was a bulletin board with notices of planes for sale, airplanes sought, offers to go in as partners on a plane, and various advisories and circulars issued by the FAA.

"Have you got any instructors who teach on week days?" I asked Paille.

"Sure," he said. "I have Tom Young. He just got his instructor's license not long ago and he helps me in the shop during the week. He'd rather be flying any day than working in the shop." Then Bill changed his tack and remarked to Bill Miller. "I'm getting to depend on Tom, you know? Tom's getting pretty good. There aren't many of them who can work on an airplane and fly it too."

We left Davis with nothing settled. I asked Bill Miller if he knew Tom Young. He said he didn't, but he didn't fly on weekdays either.

We drove to Montgomery County Air Park, a few miles from Davis. It was apparent immediately that Montgomery County is an entirely different sort of operation and facility. It is both modern and large. We only got as far as the parking lot. From there we could see the windows of the cafeteria on the second floor of the modern main building. "Costs a lot to eat here," said Bill.

"According to what Jim said in class," I remarked, "It costs a lot to fly here, too."

We returned to Aspen Hills and I thanked Bill for the tour.

For the rest of the day, I had Davis Airport on my mind. That evening, Gloria and I had friends over for dinner. I spoke of what I had seen. After dinner, we decided to see a film. I cast my vote, deciding for the lot. For me, it was a matter now of when. I knew the where of it and how. I thought I knew the why. We went to Bethesda for the seven thirty show. The Great Waldo Pepper was flying his machine.

II.

Ground school went on for two more sessions and recessed for Spring break.

FRIDAY, MARCH 28TH.

I called Davis Airport. Mrs. Paille answered the phone and told me Tom Young wasn't there, I should call back Monday.

MONDAY, MARCH 31ST.

I called back. Mrs. Paille answered again. I heard her call Tom from the shop. "It's that Mr. Doogan on the phone again," she yelled. As soon as Tom came to the phone, as soon as he had said hello, in a light tenor, nervous voice that matched my own, nasality and all, I told him I was Mr. Newcomb and not Mr. Doogan. He sounded disappointed.

A typical way in which a student engages in flight training involves an interview with a prospective instructor first of all, then a trial flight, and finally a tentative schedule. The course of things rarely runs smoothly and it is common for students to change instructors during training, and also common for a student to drop out and then resume training at a later date. But my presumptions about what I wanted had the force of thought; I presumed I knew. And Tom's presumptions had the force of confidence; he presumed to know what would be best. I proposed a schedule and Tom accepted it. I would be flying on Tuesdays and Wednesdays, in the mornings beginning at nine thirty, and on Fridays, in the afternoons, beginning at three. For me that schedule, along with ground school, filled my work-day week with general aviation.

Tom wanted to know whether I had flown before. He meant as a pilot in a small plane. I told him I had not and asked him why he wanted to know. "To see if you have any bad habits that I will have to break," he said.

"We're starting off from scratch," I said. "And how many students have you taken from the beginning right through to the end?"

"Like you said," said Tom, "We're starting off from scratch."

I convinced Tom to go for a flight that afternoon. He seemed reluctant at first but then agreed. I arrived at the airport at three thirty. The drive took forty-five minutes and the distance from home was twenty-nine miles.

Inside the office, I met Bill Paille again and Bill called to Tom to tell him I had come. "So you're going to go for it," said Bill, referring to the fact that I had arranged three lessons a week.

"I guess I am," I said, shifting my stance.

"Well, that's the way to do it," said Bill. "The more you fly the faster you learn."

Tom came into the office by the side door from the hangar, where he had been at work. He was wiping his hands on a rag. We said hello and shook hands. Tom was a husky, hale young man, open and direct. He stood six feet and weighed two hundred pounds, and his enthusiasm for flying came across immediately, with a disarming frankness that encouraged me to trust him from the start. It also wiped away whatever sense of difference I held about our respective ages, and very quickly I came to think of Tom as my elder in matters that pertained to flying. Indeed, Tom's manner was so to-the-point that at the very moment I was hoping he might say, "Let's have a cup of coffee and sit down awhile to chat," he said, instead; "Let's go," and pointed to the door.

The question what do pilots and students wear for a flying lesson had been on my mind since before I left home. The answer it appeared was to wear whatever was comfortable, and at this time of the year to dress warmly. Tom was wearing jeans and boots, a Dutzel cap and sweatshirt, with a heavy shirt over the top of that, and he wore gloves.

The Cub we were to fly today was the same one I had seen the morning I was there with Bill Miller. It sat, today as then, with its nose pointed to the parking lot, in the first tie-down of the long row of airplanes extending half the length of the runway. Nearby the Cub's right wing stood the airport's two gasoline pumps. Tom proceeded to show me around the airplane, demonstrating a pre-flight inspection that I would learn and duplicate on my own in days to come. We began at the prop. spinner, the "hub" of the propeller, to check that it was on securely. From the spinner, Tom had me run my fingertips along the leading edges of each of the two propeller blades. We were looking for nicks and cuts in the blades. To turn the propeller he had me rotate it clockwise as I faced it, a precaution, he pointed out, to keep the engine from accidentally firing, in the event the magneto switch was "hot." The lesson was impressive: the engine fires, the prop. cuts you in half. Very quickly I learned a fear of the propeller blade.

The engine of the Cub, a four cylinder, sixty-five horsepower Continental, sat exposed to view from the side. "Not much to it," said Tom, exhibiting its simplicity and small size. Then, he spotted a bolt missing from the rocker-arm panel and exclaimed, somewhat indignantly, "Now right there you see the importance of a pre-flight inspection." He left me to stare at the hole while he trekked to the hangar for a replacement part. After the repair, we checked the spark plug wires and the fuel primer.

Underneath the airplane, where the landing gear struts are hinged to the airframe, we inspected the struts for cracks in the tubular metal and welds, and the hinges for the cotter pins which hold the hinges in place. We checked the hydraulic brake lines and the tires, which seemed to me well-worn. From underneath, we moved out to the left wing, where Tom encouraged me to look at the wing in its entirety, for its shape as an airfoil, and for deformations in that shape, cuts in the fabric, nicks in the leading edge. Were I to find such things on my own I would only report the finding to Tom. But that was not the point. Tom was encouraging me to scrutinize things, to avoid that presumption, so harmful, that everything's okay. We looked at the pitot tube, which gathers impact air for the pitot-static system, thereby providing one source of pressure for the airspeed indicator. At the trailing edge of the wing, we looked at the aileron, at its control cables and hinges, and the ever-present cotter pins, which appeared to fasten all parts in place. I inspected the wing struts while Tom untied the mooring rope and pulled it through the grommet. He nudged the chock away from behind the landing gear.

We went back on our hands and knees to look at the fuselage underneath. Again, we were looking for cuts or damage to the fabric caused here, typically, by gravel thrown in the blast from the prop. Tom pointed out the static ports, which provide the pitot-static system its access to the standing pressure of the atmosphere, and so one source of pressure to the altimeter and the second source to the airspeed indicator. I was impressed by how crude this airplane was. It was so crude it was ingenious.

Tom took me aft and we inspected the rudder, the vertical stabilizer, the elevators, the horizontal stabilizers, and the guy wires that helped support them. Tom showed me the linkage on the tail wheel, which connected it to the rudder, so that wheel and rudder are commonly controlled, by cables from the rudder bars. Again, there were both safety wires and cotter pins. The whole airplane reminded me of the jitneys we used to build as kids. I removed the chain that moored the tail wheel and prevented the tail assembly from booming in the wind. Tom removed two plastic covers from openings on either side of the fuselage, where the trim system connects to the horizontal stabilizers. I was surprised to learn that these covers protected the airplane against birds, which would otherwise build nests inside the fuselage.

The cabin door opens on the right side of the airplane into upper and lower parts. Tom latched the upper door to the bottom of the wing and lowered the other half to the side of the fuselage. He stowed the bird covers in the small baggage hold behind the rear seat. The two seats in a Cub are arranged in tandem, with the flight controls duplicated, front and back. The rear stick was tied to the back of the seat in front of it by a rope, which prevented the ailerons and elevators from flapping in the wind. When I untied the stick, Tom demonstrated by working the aileron by hand, up and down, on the right wing. I watched the two sticks move left and right in unison. I checked the brakes for pressure in the line, and set the altimeter to the airport's elevation, six hundred forty feet. Tom pointed out the fuel shut-off valve, located on the lower left side of the cockpit wall, and cautioned me that the valve should remain open at all times. We resumed our tour at the right wing, and covered the same points, minus the pitot tube, which we had covered on the left. I removed the wheel chock while Tom untied the rope.

When we came to the engine again, on the right side, we checked the engine oil. Again, we inspected sparkplug wires, primer and bolts. A canvas hood cover lay draped across the fence. Tom explained that the hood was to be tied around the engine and nose of the airplane at the end of each flight, though I observed that whoever flew the Cub before us had neglected it. The hood cover protects the engine from the weather, but it serves the additional purpose of protecting it from the birds, which, Tom explained, will nest inside the engine compartment as well as in the fuselage.

The final points of the inspection concerned the fuel. The Cub has no fuel gauge as such. It has a dipstick, buoyed by a float inside the fuel tank. The dipstick protrudes through the fuel tank's cap like a stem. Unfortunately, the float had become fuel-logged and the dipstick had sunk. Tom insisted that I make a habit of knowing how much fuel was on board before each flight, but to do so by checking it visually. So, I climbed up on the tire, removed the cap from the tank which, since it sits above the level of the engine and in front of the firewall, is well above the ground, and looked in. The tank was full. Tom explained that the tank of the Cub held twelve gallons, that the Cub's engine burns four gallons an hour at cruise, and that cruise for that engine was a speed of twenty-one hundred r.p.m. "So, if you know what time it is when you take off," he postulated, "And you know how much fuel you have on board, and if you watch your r.p.m. as you go along, then you'll know how much time you'll have before the tank runs dry."

The final inspection was equally important; it involved draining the gascollator. The gascollator is a trap with a valve, located at the lowest point in the fuel line. Since water is denser than gasoline, whatever water should condense, from the humidity of the air, and form inside the fuel tank, will settle to the bottom of the tank, or the lowest point in the fuel line. Draining the gascollator allows the pilot to check for condensate, and clear it if it formed.

The Cub was ready to go. Tom instructed me on the technique for pushing it, since we had to roll it backwards from its berth, and from there across the service area to the grass along the eastern end of the runway. To push an airplane of this size would appear difficult, but it is not. The Cub weighs only eight hundred pounds, in spite of its thirty-foot wingspan, sixteen-foot length, and six-and-a-half-foot height. The skin of the airplane is fabric, coated with airplane dope, easily punctured or torn. To protect against that, Tom had me push with the flats of my hands against the leading edges of the vertical and horizontal stabilizers.

When the airplane rolled to a stop, Tom began an introduction to its instruments and flight controls, what few of those there were. Here, I thought I knew everything there was to know, and I interrupted his remarks by saying, "Yes," or adding, "I know," or "I know that."

Finally, it broke his rhythm. He said, "Okay, what should the oil temperature gauge read?"

I shut my mouth.

"It won't read anything," he said. "The engine runs too cool." Then he pointed out the oil pressure gauge and advised me on yet another cardinal rule - the rules were beginning to mount up - that if the gauge has not shown pressure within thirty seconds after starting the engine in hot weather, or sixty seconds in cold, then shut the engine down at once. He proceeded to the next gauge, the tachometer, which sat on the left of the panel and completed the group of three engine-monitoring instruments. Below the gauges was the fuel primer pump, and below the panel, the carburetor heat valve.

Mounted above the panel in the center sat the magnetic compass, the only direction-seeking instrument on the airplane. On the panel to the left of the compass were the altimeter and airspeed indicator, plus the one gyro instrument on board, the turn and slip indicator. "See those doghouses?" Tom said, pointing to marks shaped like doghouses to either side of center on the gauge. "Those indicate a standard rate turn. How fast is that?"

"Three degrees per second," I said.

"Very good," said Tom. "And what is the name for a standard rate turn through a full circle?"

"A two minute turn," I answered.

"That's good, very good," said Tom. "Now get aboard."

"Front seat or back?"

"The pilot sits in back." Since he motioned toward the back I took it that meant me. Boarding a Cub the first time proved no bargain. There was very little to hold on to and I had the feeling that if I grabbed the wrong thing the airplane would collapse. Once inside, there was very little room to move about. The rear seat of the Cub forms a wedge, seat-back and seat-bottom, and the sense that I was sitting too low, with my knees too high, that I was wedged-in, as it were, was compounded by the angle of the airplane, which itself sat nose-high. "Did you study weight and balance?" Tom asked.

"Yes we did," I said, ready to add how well I scored on the test.

"Then you should know," he said, "That if you're flying solo in this plane, and you're sitting in the front seat, the airplane will be nose heavy and you'll have a hard time flaring out to land."

Since I was facing uphill, my view forward was obstructed by the airplane itself. I could see the cockpit, of course, the instrument panel, the hood of the engine, the windshield compass, fuel dipstick, prop. blade and sky. It occurred to me that the airplane landed this way, three-points, nose high. How do you see the runway when you land?

I was looking about at everything, since everything was new. "Put your seat belt on," said Tom. "Always the first thing." I groped for the seat belt. Tom began showing me the throttles. Things were beginning to move slightly too fast now for me to keep up with him. "Any questions?" he asked. I told him no. "Right hand holds the stick," he said. "Left band holds the throttle. Gently now." I tried to follow what he said, but things began to move too fast. "You hold the knob of the throttle between your index finger and your thumb. You pinch. Just firmly enough to make adjustments." He showed me the rudder pedals. I was still fiddling with the throttle when he began to show me the brakes. Heels onto the brakes; balls of the feet on the rudder. He pointed out the magneto switch. I was still concerned with the rudder and the brakes. I snapped my head around to catch up to him. By my temple, on the left side wall above the window was the switch. I definitely had begun to feel cramped. By my feet I caught glimpses of the control cables, running fore to aft along the floor. The floor was plywood; I noticed that now.

Tom began demonstrating the primer pump. He primed the engine and told me to finish. I could barely reach around the seat in front to get to the handle. Already, Tom began showing me the trim. The trim crank, to the left on the side wall by the front seat, also proved difficult to reach. I was wedged too far down in my seat; my own knees got in my way. There was no room to straighten out my legs. "You'll get used to it," said Tom. "Crank forward for nose down; backward for nose up. The trim stays neutral for the take-off now. Any questions?"

"No questions," I said, and Tom moved away from the door and out of my view, forward, in front of the prop.

"Stick back," he called.

I held the stick back, as far as it would go, almost to my belly, and saw that my arm had begun to tremble. "Stick back," I yelled to Tom, and realized that I was out of breath.

"Brakes on," he called. I found the brakes and dug my heels in.

"Brakes on," I answered back to him. My eyes found a placard: for airworthiness and owner's registration.

"Switch off," Tom yelled.

"Switch off," I said right back at him. There were placards posted for weight and balance, engine r.p.m., top speed.

"Throttle closed," said Tom.

"Throttle closed," I echoed back. No radio. No radio navigation. "No smoking," said the sign.

The airplane shook and I saw the propeller turn. There was a sound of the valves, the pistons in the engine, fuel being drawn. The airplane shook a second time and the prop. blade came around again. I could see Tom's fingertips on the edge of the blade, flits of images of his elbows and shoulders. He wound up and came down like a pitcher throwing home. The prop. swung around again. The engine made a chug. "Okay," he yelled, "Switch on both."

I cranked the magneto switch from "Off" to "Both." My heels remained dug in tight on the brakes. My right arm ached from holding back the stick. "On both," I yelled.

"Contact," yelled Tom, and one more time he pulled the engine through. The prop. spun, the engine fired and ran. The airplane began to vibrate immediately throughout and my ears filled with the engine's awesome noise.

Tom ducked under the wing struts and climbed aboard. "Oil pressure," he said, and I looked in time to see the needle of the gauge begin to rise. With Tom in front of me now, my view of the world was even further blocked, and my view of the instruments was replaced by the sight of the back of his head, his neck and shoulders, and his Dutzel cap. He pulled up the bottom door and pulled down the top, then latched them both together closed.

"'Why do I hold the stick back?" I asked, shouting, as all exchanges would be from here on out.

"To keep the prop. blast from lifting the tail off the ground," he shouted back. "Any more questions?" I shook my head. "All set?" I nodded. "Then do the run-up test," he said.

I did as he instructed me, and nudged the throttle forward. No sooner had the engine begun to build up speed than the airplane shifted slightly on the ground. By reflex I nailed the brakes, a panic stop. I pushed the throttle forward more. The tachometer settled at fifteen hundred. I ran the mag. switch through to the left magneto. The engine's speed fell off slightly. The tachometer showed a drop to fourteen-fifty. "On both," said Tom. I put the switch on both again. The engine resumed its fifteen hundred turns. "Right mag.," Tom said. I turned the switch one click. The engine speed fell off and the tachometer registered fourteen-seventy. I returned the switch to both once more. "Carb. heat," said Tom. In a cumbersome exchange of grips I managed to trade the stick from my right hand to my left, then tried reaching around Tom and Tom's seat to get at the carburetor heat valve. I tried to keep both feet on the brakes. I gnashed my teeth. When I pulled the heat valve on, no change occurred in the engine's pitch. "It's not warmed up enough to show a change," said Tom.

I pulled the throttle back to idle.

"Just follow through with what I do," Tom said and took the controls away from me. With great relief I relinquished my grasp on the stick, which Tom began to work now easily, left and right, backward and forward, to check the flight controls.

Tom throttled up again. The airplane rolled onto the blacktop of the service area and swung around to the left, facing the runway. We stopped. He checked the approach, to our left to see that no planes were coming in to land. Then he nudged the throttle again and we rolled forward onto the runway. The tail swung around and we turned again, to the right, into the wind now and aligned with the bearing of the runway. The runway out ahead of me was gone from view, replaced by the sight of the airplane's nose, and Tom.

I watched as the throttle moved forward, all the way to its stop; I watched the stick move forward to a neutral position. I had the sense the airplane was doing this itself. The sound of the engine rose to a considerable roar and the ship began rolling, faster very quickly, with vibrations and jouncing spreading throughout. The propeller blast combed the cockpit, finding the seams in the windshield and walls. I looked out the window to the left; the grass and margin of the runway zipping by. Then the Cub sashayed once, as if we had stepped on ice and lost our footing. The side of the runway slid away. The ride became suddenly firm. The taxi strip and runway light descended from my view; the whole periphery began to drop. The nose of the Cub rode up high. We were off the ground and climbing out.

My heart was so much in a rush, as well as all my senses, that my mind, recording deeds my eyes had seen, my senses known, just relayed what was happening and left all thought of things behind. The major perception of motion occurred in gaps and frames: You look one place, you're here. You look someplace else, you're almost there. You look back to the first place, and you're gone, already past. We were over trees. Now we were turning. We were over a sub-division. Now we were turning. We were over a field and a farm. I looked below the right wing and I saw the airport, well below and far away. I felt as though I were aboard a boat, a small boat, just putting out on a slightly swelling sea. The horizon provided us with reference now, for it had become just that, unbroken save for the intrusion of Sugar Loaf Mountain to the west of us; unbroken in a level line. It passed my mind how seldom I had seen a true horizon.

Tom levelled the airplane at eighteen hundred feet. Sugar Loaf seemed near, within reachable distance out ahead of the plane, though I ought to have known it was several miles away. The airspeed indicator showed our speed was sixty-five. The air remained calm, but I was sensitive to every tipping from an even keel. I wanted by my instincts to clutch at some support. Yet, at the same time, I felt exhilaration. The wind, so audible on the wings and in the struts, found a way into the cracks around the doors and the windows. It made a very pleasant sound. Exhilaration. The engine seemed not so forbidding now, less loud but constant, still loud but in a drone.

Tom turned in his seat and asked me what I thought. I told him I felt like a kid. He asked if I would like to fly the ship. I told him yes. He gave me my points of reference: how the horizon looked, cutting across the windshield at the level of the compass, how it looked below the tips of the wings. "If the wind tips us up, correct for it with ailerons," he said. I nodded that I understood. "It's yours," he said. I took the plane away from him.

We turned northwesterly when we reached Interstate 270. I

should have known where we were precisely, but I didn't. I was still riding the tremendous surge of exuberance, and lacked the mind to reason or deduce. Even Tom, who knew the terrain and had flown over it so many times, caught my excitement, shared in my discoveries, and became as enthusiastic about going to an old place as I was going to a new one.

I committed a usual run of errors. I overcontrolled the airplane and gripped the controls too tightly. I looked too long in any one direction and failed to scan. Tom told me to move my eyes across the horizon, check the wing tips, left and right, sweep the instruments. But it was new. He understood. I began to develop some bad habits as well. I kept riding with the left wing a little low. Even after I corrected it, I soon lapsed into it again. And I failed to scan the altimeter as a part of the routine. We had lost two hundred feet before I was aware we had.

I noticed that the sky looked dirty, an odd observation since, from the ground, the sky looked clear. There were no clouds, but the horizon was smudged by a rim of brown haze. "Fifteen miles visibility," said Tom "Not too much for a cloudless day in March."

I was also surprised to observe the effects of the wind on our ground speed. We were following the line of the freeway below and while our airspeed remained at sixty-five, the effects of the headwind, quartering from the west, had reduced our ground speed so much that the traffic on the freeway was leaving us behind. Moreover, to keep from drifting to the right of our course, I found we had to head to the left of our course by ten or more degrees.

Outskirts of the town of Frederick began to emerge from the distance out ahead. "Ever been to Frederick?" yelled Tom.

"No," I yelled back. "Only by it."

"Not so easy to fly straight and level, is it?"

"No," I yelled, "I never thought it would be." Tom took over the controls and I discovered I was clearly tired. My right arm ached. I believe I told a lie to Tom, for I had thought that flying would be like apple pie for me.

Frederick's municipal airport appeared, a much larger airport than Davis. There were two bisecting runways, and the runways themselves seemed huge from the air. Tom asked if I could see the windsock or the T. As we passed over the boundary of the airport, I spotted them both. It was as the book had promised it would be.

"What's the active runway?" Tom yelled back. I looked down at the T. It indicated a landing south, opposite the direction we were heading now. I looked at the runway we were to use but could not make out the numbers, upside down to me and still at a distance, "What say?" asked Tom. I looked at the compass, to get a clue, but the compass was swinging wildly. Tom pulled the carburetor heat on and pulled the throttle back. The Cub started down. "I'm waiting," he said.

We rolled into a turn, around to the right. The runway swept by to the left, around and out of sight behind the plane. How difficult to think reasonably and fly at the same time. We were moving away from the approach end now. "Yes?" asked Tom, and he rolled the Cub into another right turn, beginning our entry into the pattern. The southern end of the runway came around into view, lying ahead off the port side of the Cub's nose. Those numbers, painted large and white, I could see clearly. Runway 01, if used north. Then we would land on the reciprocal end of runway 01. What was the reciprocal of 01?

"What is pattern altitude?" asked Tom.

"What's the airport elevation?" I replied.

"Three hundred feet," he said.

"Eleven hundred feet," I replied.

"What runway are we landing on?" he asked.

"What's the reciprocal of runway 01?" I asked.

"What?"

"Nineteen, I think."

"Nineteen it is. You must be doing good in school."

"I used to think I was," I answered him.

Tom pulled the throttle back to idle. He cranked in the trim as the airspeed dropped to fifty and we started the glide of our approach. We passed the threshold of the runway, which lay out to the left of the plane, below the wing, and continued on northbound, descending in the glide, opposite the direction we would land. Then Tom rolled us into a turn, ninety degrees to the left onto the base leg of the approach, so that, when the Cub levelled again, the runway lay ahead and to the left of us. He rolled the Cub through a second turn, ninety degrees to the left again, and we entered our final approach, the runway dead ahead of us and the numbers, 19, right side up at last. Details of the earth became apparent once again. The runway flattened out, what I could see of it coming up around us from the sides. Then Tom flared the Cub, and boom; we were down. "I bounced it," he reported.

"Seemed good to me," I said. The Cub slowed and pulled off the runway to the right, onto the margin of grass.

"Bounced it," Tom repeated, and swung us around to face the runway as we stopped. "Well," he said, "What do you think now?"

I looked to the right, down several thousand feet of runway to the hangar and the administration building. Then I looked to the left, to the threshold we just passed. "You only used four hundred feet to land."

The return trip was direct and swift. We had a quartering tail wind to boost us, so our ground speed now was ten or fifteen miles an hour higher than our airspeed. Tom let me fly again while he pointed out some landmarks on the way. We followed the general course of a country road, whose actual path doglegged back and forth beneath the plane. The road extended from a drag strip near Frederick to the town of Damascus, some fourteen miles to the east, south-east. Damascus became a major checkpoint, and would provide in the future a sure sign to home. The only shopping center in the area took up a segment of the town. More appealing was the town's church. Its steeple stood out in the bright afternoon, bright white, pointed, visible for miles. The road that ran out from town, beginning at the church, led us straight on a line to Davis. From two miles away, I could see the wings of parked airplanes, glinting in the sun.

After we were down, Tom taxied the Cub right into its berth. "Switch off," he said. I turned the mag. switch off and the engine quickly died. I found, on getting out, that my legs had become stiff and I had trouble standing up. I also took note that it suddenly seemed too still. I found I continued to want to shout instead of speak. I had the sound of seashells in my ears. Then, too, it seemed the ground I stood on was shifting underneath my feet.

While I marveled at physiology, Tom went to work. The end of a flight, like the end of a ride in a boat, requires some work to be done by the crew. I was the crew. But, today, Tom excused me from work, because, as he observed, he thought I looked a little goofy. The last thing he did was tie the hood around the engine of the plane.

Inside the office he marked down the gas we used - 3.6 gallons - and sold me a log book and an air chart. Tom made the first entry in my book. I marvelled at the entry. I was a pilot. My first hour of dual.

Bill Paille came out from the hangar. "Well, how'd it go?" he said.

"Good," I said.

"Is he Air Force material?" he asked Tom.

"Sure is," said Tom, the punch line for the hype.

TUESDAY, APRIL 1ST.

Today began the first of my regular lessons. I arrived at the airport at nine thirty. Again the weather was fair, the sun bright, the sky cloudless.

Tom had me check out the Cub by myself today. What we discussed yesterday about birds came to mind again after I untied the hood cover and draped it over the fence. A bird's egg fell from the engine compartment and broke on the ground. When I looked inside the engine compartment I could hear a rustle and see pieces of the nest. Then the bird flew out and brushed my face.

Tom merely shrugged at the news. With a whisk broom in one hand and a screwdriver in the other, he trudged out to the Cub, removed the cowling, and swept away the remainder of the nest.

When the Cub was ready, we repeated the routine for starting the engine and running it up. On the take-off, once we cleared the runway, Tom gave me the controls to let me fly the ship. "Hold your heading," he said; when he recognized we no longer followed the imaginary extension of the runway's centerline but had begun to drift. "Hold your airspeed," he said, when he recognized I was changing the nose-up, nose-down pitch. "Look at your wingtips," he said, which meant I had let the wingtips dip, by degrees imperceptible to me, to the left or to the right, which turned the plane.

I made ready to start the turn to the left, from the upwind leg to the crosswind leg of the pattern. All at once, Tom yelled at me and grabbed the stick away. He shoved the nose down and rolled us to the right. A huge, lazy crow flapped by the windshield, missing us, and missing the propeller, by just a yard. It seemed this was my day for birds.

"If you're going to fly the airplane," Tom yelled, "You've got to be in charge from the very minute you start the engine."

"Okay," I said, "But I couldn't see the crow."

"You have to look."

What I did see was that the sky was treacherous in the same way that Melville said the sea was treacherous: that beauty was the mask for sudden harm.

Once we departed the pattern, we turned west and held eighteen hundred feet on a course toward Sugar Loaf. We began work on level turns. The mistakes I had made for the first time yesterday, I began to make habitually today. I failed to scan, I failed to hold altitude, I rode with the left wing low. I continued an exhibit of nervousness, I overcontrolled.

Practice became montonous, drawn out by mistakes that recurred. No sooner did I finish a left turn of three hundred sixty degrees at thirty degrees of bank, with the hope of rolling out of the turn on a heading toward Sugar Loaf, only to see that I had missed the roll-out by rolling past my heading, than Tom put me through a right turn, three hundred sixty degrees as well, at the same degree of bank, and I missed the right turn, too, allowing the altitude to drop a hundred feet while turning. I allowed the banks to steepen too far, to forty,

forty-five degrees, then jerked the controls to reduce the bank and, as a result, would come out of the turn short of the heading, by ten or fifteen degrees.

We did it again, and we did it again and again. Establish the heading. Establish the altitude. Ease the stick over and roll into a bank. Look out on the wing. See where the fairing came up to the horizon. Hold the bank. Neutralize the ailerons. Play in with the rudder. Get off the rudder. Come back on the stick. Watch altitude. Hold steady. Watch references, the needle, the ball of the turn and slip indicator, the horizon, the pasturelands turning below. Then start the roll-out. Opposite ailerons, opposite rudder, ease off the back-pressure on the stick. Until, finally, one came right, bingo, right on the heading, and Sugar Loaf stood out ahead.

We proceeded to work on glides. We came down, with the power off, the carburetor heat on, the trim cranked in, to hold the airspeed down, at fifty as we snaked through turns, ninety degrees to the left, ninety degrees to the right. Even with the help of trim, the amount of back-pressure I held, the strenuous, constant, constantly changing effort to control the stick, caused my right arm to ache, with a hot point of pain in the muscles of the shoulder. Having glided down through a series of turns, Tom had me climb back up to altitude through another series. The Cub took its time, poking along at fifty, its rate of climb very low. We climbed, turning to the right, and continued to climb, turning to the left. The altimeter crept around. We reached eighteen hundred feet and continued beyond that to twenty-five hundred before Tom said level out. He told me to hold altitude and start pulling the power back. I watched the altimeter and began coming back on the throttle. "Hold fifteen hundred r.p.m.," said Tom. That seemed unnatural to me, insufficient to keep us at that height. I had become accustomed to a certain sound of the engine in level flight, a certain attitude of the airplane's nose. Now, the Cub rode nose up high, as if we were climbing, though we weren't. The controls became soft in their responses. The airplane seemed tipsy and began to wallow. I retracted the throttle, by degrees more. I watched the tachometer. I watched the airspeed indicator. The stick became softer still. I came back harder on it to force the nose up higher. The ship became unstable. The pointers of the altimeter held fast at twenty-five hundred. The airplane was going to tumble. I felt we were doing a balancing act, on top of a soft rubber ball. The wind tipped us. My feeling of a solid foundation was gone. My instincts made me look for new supports, for things to hold. I had the stick to hold, and the throttle in my other hand. "Comfortable?" Tom asked.

"Of course," I shouted, my second flagrant lie. "What next?"

"Pull the carb. heat on," he said.

I tried reaching around his seat to get the carb. heat knob. I exchanged my grips on the stick, afraid to let go of anything. The engine slowed when the heat was applied. It seemed the propeller was barely turning, that we dangled by a thread. "Come back on the stick some more," said Tom.

"I can't."

"Why not? Come back."

I came back on the stick a fraction of a millimeter, a hundredth of an ounce more pressure from my hand.

"Come back," he said.

I had to trust him now. I came back on the stick. My childhood dread of rollercoaster rides recurred. The nose rode up, up. The horizon fell away below us. Things grew calm. The wind subsided. The airplane creaked, teetered once, and went over the brink.

The earth rose, filling the entire windshield, until the landscape spread before us like a map. My stomach rose to my throat, "Let off the throttle, let off the stick!" yelled Tom. I let off the throttle, I let off the stick. He pulled the throttle closed; "Pull out!" he yelled. I grabbed the stick again and hauled it back. The airplane zoomed, the response of the stick solid now, hefty again, and we came out of the dive. I looked at the altimeter; it had unwound like a sprung clock and taken back four hundred feet. The airspeed had risen from thirty-five to ninety. Now it settled down again. My stomach settled down again. The horizon and the map of earth receded to their normal plane again. Tom started adding power as the airspeed dropped to sixty-five.

"How steep did we just dive?" I asked.

"Don't let the nose down so far next time," he said.

"How steep?"

"How steep is seventy-five degrees?"

At the end of the flight when I climbed out of the airplane I discovered I had become weak-kneed. I had not reckoned until then with how physical, how visceral, my responses to flight would be. I should have known it was not done in your mind but in your sense of fear, which for me came from my bowels. Tom was sympathetic, but only to the extent that he allowed me to sit for a moment in the grass beside the plane. He did not excuse me from chores. "Almost everyone feels that way during the first few stalls," he said. "By tomorrow you will take it right in stride."

After I finished tying down the airplane and refueling the tank I went to the office. There, Tom introduced me to Orville White, who worked in the shop part-time for Bill. While I stood, looking over Tom's shoulder as Tom wrote an entry in my log, Orville offered to buy a round of Cokes. This caused Tom to start. "You treating?" Tom asked.

"I'm treating," Orville answered, and looked from Tom to me.

"No thanks," I said.

"You better take him up on, it," said Tom. "You'll never hear that offer made again."

WEDNESDAY, APRIL 2ND.

For the third day, the weather was fair. Tom advised me that we would continue to work on stalls today, as well as turns. It put me in a proper frame of mind, grim.

During the climb-out Tom gave me the airplane again to fly, as he had done yesterday. This time I was appreciably more intent on looking out. Today, nothing happened. For a moment, at two thousand feet, as we headed toward Sugar Loaf again, we entered a layer of calm air. For the duration of that moment nothing seemed to move. The airplane flew all by itself, in perfect trim.

Later Tom would remind me of that moment, as evidence that I worked the flight controls too hard.

We resumed our practice of turns, beginning with banks of thirty degrees and progressing to turns with steeper banks of forty-five degrees. The measures of success were to roll out of each turn directly on the heading, which was Sugar Loaf again, and to maintain altitude in the conduct of the turn. I graduated from single turns to seven hundred twenty degree turns, two times around, and would have become disoriented if it had not been for the mountain as a reference. We reviewed climb-turns, holding fifty miles an hour, and gliding turns, holding fifty miles an hour. We practiced ninety-degree turns, left and right in close order, at forty-five degrees bank.

At last we went back to "mushing" again, flight at critically slow airspeed, with the engine throttled down to fifteen hundred r.p.m. Tom had me nurse the airplane around a three hundred sixty degree turn to the left at that speed, and told me not to lose altitude during the turn. I lost a hundred fifty feet and told him it was not possible to do. He did one, to show me that it was. He did one turn to the left, and held the altitude, then did a second turn to the right and climbed two hundred feet. "Economy," he said, "You just don't waste motion."

I began to learn, even if only by the memory of sequence. I began to expect things to happen, and to correct for them as they did. We began to work on stalls. We entered each stall by cutting the power and then coming back on the stick. Tom wanted me to overcome my apprehension so that I would register the sensations rather than my fear of them. When the sensations began to be predictable at last, my queasiness subsided. I began to pick up the tell-tale signs, the feel of the ship on the verge of the stall. In that way, we could play with the stall, fly at critically slow airspeeds, remain on the brink and not go over, or go over and recover fast. First, I did the stalls power off, then I did them power on, from fifteen hundred r.p.m. Either way, the recovery included adding power, letting the nose down, but not too far below the horizon's line, then, when flying speed returned to us, leveling out again. I continued to want to let the nose drop down too far, the airplane dive.

When Tom felt satisfied that I was making progress with the straight-ahead stall he introduced the stall, that comes in the midst of a turn. We did them left and right. I tended to overbank, a condition the airplane will not tolerate when it flies on the verge of a stall. It counters with a tendency to spin. We almost spun out to the high side of the turn on two occasions, and each time I pleased Tom by correcting for the tendency before the spin began. "I'm getting good." I yelled to Tom.

"You are?" he yelled.

"I can correct for a spin." I said.

"Is that right?" he answered back. "Got your seat belt tight?" he said.

I told him that I did, and laughed. He laughed, too, then rolled the airplane over into a bank to the right. The bank steepened and steepened until I could look directly out the right side and directly down the wing, which now pointed directly to the earth, where I could see a farm pond, which seemed to be fixed as we spun around, on the point of the wing, two thousand feet below us. Centrifugal force crammed me into my seat. "Oh brother," dribbled from my lips. More than I had reckoned for. Suddenly, the airplane breeched and the nose swung straight up into the air. We were vertical, standing on our tail. The airplane fell over to the left and the world inverted and went around. It went around again. "Correct for the spin," yelled Tom.

"I can't!"

He rolled us level and we flew away.

After we landed, we sat on the rail of the fence and ate our lunches from the brown bags each of us had brought. I mentioned to Tom how much I had enjoyed the stalls we did today. He noticed that I didn't finish lunch. The late morning sun was bright, and the air of April, cool. We talked admiringly of the men and planes of World

War II. Finally, I asked Tom if he wanted to fly some more that afternoon. Tom needn't be asked that. The question was, did I? Orville came out to join us on our break. He remarked that I looked a little peaked. "I just spun one out over the top," said Tom. Orville thought that was the funniest thing he had ever heard.

We were not airborne long the second time out before I showed signs of the fatigue I had been denying. It showed up in my flying, which was ragged. I had not as yet gauged the intensity of flight, or the extent to which an hour and a half of flying would drain me of reserves.

We flew east this time and Tom pointed out the countryside between Davis and Tridelphia Reservoir. Most of the land was farm land, much less of it developed into the subdivisions so conspicuous from the air above Interstate 270, our route to the west. Tom picked out a rectangular farm field and introduced a maneuver called "rectangular courses." I flew around the field making left hand turns. We held to an altitude seven hundred feet above the ground. The point of the practice was to maintain a constant altitude and constant distance from the perimeter of the field. At one corner, there were children at play in an adjacent yard. They became quite absorbed in watching us as we flew by overhead, again and again. The difficulty of the maneuver lay in correcting for wind drift, and anticipating the drift before and during the turns. I found that after two times around the field in one direction, I was no longer able to remember or sense from where the wind was coming. I had become disoriented. Reversing our course to do the turns in the opposite direction made it even worse. I began to curse myself for my ineptitude. I began to fight the airplane, too, and wrestle it through the turns. "You're tired," said Tom. We broke off. Tom wanted to go back. "You've had it for the day," he said.

"No I haven't," I insisted.

We flew on. Tom located an open field near the reservoir. He was going to have me find out for myself. In the middle of the field stood a small tree, which would serve as a reference point in another ground reference maneuver. The maneuver, called "turns about a point," was like rectangular courses in that its practice helped a pilot cope with drift. The idea was to fly around the point in a circle of constant radius, at a constant altitude, about seven hundred feet above the ground.

Tom demonstrated the maneuver and explained it as we went. We entered, flying downwind, the bush ahead of us, below and to the right. He banked into a right-hand turn. The bush became centered within the frame of the struts on the right wing. As we came around downwind he compensated for the tendency of the wind to blow us away by tightening the turn. As we came upwind, our ground speed lessened, so Tom reduced the angle of bank, by degrees, to lessen the rate of our turn. Upwind, the bank was least. This kept the wind from blowing us in over the top of the bush. As Tom did this, I followed through on the controls. It seemed easy. Tom took us twice around and then gave the controls to me. Within half a turn I forgot where the wind was coming from, and let it blow us in over the top of the bush. The perfect circles Tom's track described became, in my hands, oblong oddities of mangled oval form. "Where's the bush?" I would cry, as the bush disappeared behind the wing, or out of sight behind the fuselage.

When Tom had me break off and fly upwind, to reverse course and come back at the bush again, now with turns to be made to the left, I became disoriented over the peninsulas of the reservoir and couldn't find the field or the bush. "Agree with me you're tired," said Tom.

"I'm tired," I said, "Now where's the bush?"

"It's underneath the plane."

*   *   *

One curious effect of flying remained with me during the twenty-four hours that followed Wednesday's lesson. It was the airman's equivalent of "sea legs." Every time I sat down, the chair beneath me seemed to move. If I shut my eyes, I could imagine, with no trouble, that I was in the Cub.

THURSDAY, APRIL 3RD.

A storm system passed through New England, and even in Washington, three hundred miles from the center of the low, we suffered rains and the highest winds in local weather history. The winds ranged at sixty miles an hour all afternoon, with gusts that peaked at seventy-five. The damage was colossal.

In the evening, I forged through winds of forty miles an hour to get to school. Powerlines were down, trees were down, too. Branches were strewn everywhere and traffic was backed up for miles. Jim announced other casualties as well. During spring break, two of our members had dropped out. Of the two, I only knew Posie Preston to say hello, I didn't know the other man at all.

We were beginning meteorology in class. The weather of the day was at least appropriate to that. I looked for Bill Miller, but, of course, he was absent. The PEPCO crews would be out all day and night. No one seemed to have much mind for talking shop.

Jim promised that either we would love meteorology or we would loathe it. He said he made that guess from past experience. When I realized that the text glossed over its treatment of weather *per se* and concentrated instead on the symbology of weather; that is, the study of the study of the weather, or, how to get a weather briefing, I joined the group that did not care for it. The language of a weather briefing is codified to the point where no language at all is spoken. Even the phrase, "Weather Information," is coded by the symbol, "WX." Symbol systems are nothing if not manipulable. The National Weather Service changes the rules that govern the format of its briefings quite frequently, and much of what we learned in class was quickly obsolete.

Weather conditions are reported or predicted in different sets, according to the use a pilot plans to make of them. Hour Sequence Reports provide the kind of information a pilot may need, pertinent to current weather at selected points within a region. That may include degree of cloud cover and height of ceiling, strength and direction of surface winds, barometric pressure and its tendency to rise or fall, the temperature, visibility, and the nature of the current weather-making phenomena, thunderstorms, sleet, hail, dust, haze, etc. There are also forecasts for winds aloft and temperatures, at different altitudes, from different reporting points Those are useful in navigation for determining drift, heading, ground speed.

In addition to the teletype print-outs, there are charts that a pilot can look at to see, first-hand, the development of fronts, air masses, highs and lows, ridges and troughs. There are depictions for the kinds of clouds, which include more than thirty variations of the three basic cloud forms, cumulus, stratus, and cirrus. There are low-level and high-level prognostications, covering long-ranges or short-ranges of time. And there is the time scale itself: everything is measured by Greenwich Mean Time, itself a symbolic concept, further abbreviated to "GMT," which is re-symbolized as "Zulu Time," which, in turn, abbreviates again to "Zulu"

FRIDAY. APRIL 4TH.

The winds remained at forty miles an hour. I called Tom to see how he was. He reported that the airplanes were all flying on their ropes. One broke a wing.

MONDAY, APRIL 7TH.

We continued studying weather. The winds continued too. Bill Miller came to class tonight. I spoke with him at length during recess. He said he had had about six hours sleep the last five days. He was pleased when I told him I was flying. "So you're a five hour wonder," he said. It occurred to me that I was beginning to sound like the rest of the malarky artists in our class. Bill remarked that he was far behind in his studies but had plans to make a surge and catch up. After recess, Jim ran us through practice briefings. It was alternately funny and embarrassing as we stumbled over the codes. Even the commercial students, who had been through this for years, fared none too well. After class, Nutwell asked me if I had soloed yet.

TUESDAY, APRIL 8TH.

For the sixth day, the winds continued strong from the north. That did not seem to bother Tom. Both of us were wearing winter clothes today.

Tom began to teach me the technique for pulling the prop. through in order to start the engine of the Cub. Technique was involved, for reasons of safety. He positioned me in front of the propeller, on the left as I faced the airplane. The propeller turns counterclockwise as I faced it (clockwise from the point of view of the plane). He had me stand, not quite an arm's length from the blade, and to stand with my feet at shoulder width apart. From that substantially balanced position, he had me place both hands on the blade before me, which we had rotated to head height, and to rest my fingertips along the top, trailing edge, of the blade. My hands were a third of the way out from the root of the blade. That represented a compromise - the hands being far enough away from the root of the blade to impart leverage to the turn, yet near enough in to follow through. As I pulled the blade down and around, I kicked back with my left foot. The momentum of the kick carried my body a step or two away, backwards, to give clearance in case the engine should start and the brakes not hold the plane. I tried a few, with the switch off and Tom supervising. It took considerable power to pull the prop. around with any authority. The few I tried I got it half-way around. The engine barely turned. Tom showed me one. He pulled it through and the engine turned three times.

Tom climbed aboard and we picked up our procedure, this time with me calling and Tom responding. "Brakes on," I called.

"Brakes on," Tom said.

I pushed against the root of the prop.; the airplane held. "Switch off," I yelled.

"Switch off," said Tom.

"Throttle closed," I said.

"Throttle closed," he answered back.

"Stick back."

"Stick back." I heard him prime the engine. I pulled the prop. through twice. Adrenalin began to surge.

"Switch on," I called.

"Switch on," he called. "Contact!"

"Contact!" I ripped the prop. around. The engine started up at once. I could not have been surprised, yet the thrust of my leg carried me backwards fifteen feet, backpedaling all the way. I heard Tom laugh. As I came around, giving very wide clearance to the propeller, and ducked underneath the wing to climb aboard, he said, "I see that you regard it as a sword."

"No, I don't," I said, "A guillotine."

We took off on runway 26, with a ninety degree crosswind from our right. After we left the pattern we flew east again to work on ground reference maneuvers. The wind was ideal.

Tom picked out the same farm field we had used the week prior to fly rectangular courses. My concentration was so single-minded that the experience of the pattern, around the field, left turn after left turn, became very nearly hypnotic. I could see the line of the field, the furrows turned over, the grass in sprouts, tufts along the field fence, the turn, the drainage ditch along the roadside. The house came up, the driveway, barn, the tractor sitting out, the turn again. Down the next line of fence to the corner where the yard lay, where the children played a week ago and watched us overhead. Everything became framed by the reference of the wing and struts. I let the altitude lapse. I was not flying at all, not attending to the flight, but rather to maneuvering the imagery below, to make things fit inside the picture frame of struts against the bottom of the wing. The tension in my hand retracted the throttle by degrees. I did not notice. The engine's speed dropped off to nineteen hundred r.p.m. I had not heard. We were coming down, and I was unaware of that. "Any time now," said Tom.

I scanned the instruments, saw the altimeter and tachometer, put the power on again and climbed.

We broke off from practice and flew on across the countryside until Tom found another farm, suitable, away from houses. In the middle of a pasture we found a tree that would serve as a center to our turns about a point. I began them to the right, then reversed and came back to do them to the left. Disorientation set upon me, the effect of single mindedness again. Without a sense of where the wind was coming from, I had no feeling for the turn. I was reacting now, without anticipation. The wind was rough, turbulent, and continually upset my banks. I lost my rudder coordination and began slipping inside the turns, then overcorrecting and skidding to the outside. "Watch the ball," said Tom, referring me to the ball of the turn and slip indicator, whose path to the bottom of the turn meant slip; to the top, outside, meant skid.

"I can't," I said, "I can't watch everything at once."

"You will," said Tom, "You'll have no choice when I'm not here." I recognized that Tom was right. He could have read off items as a litany, for sport: altitude, airspeed, r.p.m.; engine oil pressure, temperature, turn and slip; watch the horizon, watch the wings, watch the references on the ground, watch out for other planes. Keep a weather eye. Know fuel amounts and time. Then fly the plane, by the stick, throttle, rudder. Set the trim. I knew the less of it I did myself the more I trusted to dumb luck.

When we broke off for the day and headed back to Davis, I caught myself in just this type of error. I would have thought we had been flying for maybe forty minutes. I had not watched the time. We had been up for an hour and forty minutes.

When we entered the downwind leg for the landing, Tom pointed out the windsock and added that the wind had picked up somewhat since we left. The sock was standing nearly straight out on the mast and still perpendicular to the direction we would land. On base leg the Cub's engine almost quit. It had iced up, even with the carburetor heat applied. The engine sputtered and the prop. slowed down so much I could see the blade tips spin. Tom nudged the throttle. The engine came to life again.

On base leg, we were flying directly into the wind. Our airspeed remained at fifty, but it was obvious we were hanging in the air, descending with very little progress. Tom added power, to stretch the glide. We turned to final and he pulled the power off. The wind came directly from our right side now. He dropped the right wing, jammed in the left rudder, and we slipped, down in a rush, tilted sideways and buffeting. He pulled the stick. We flared out and dropped on hard. "Bounced it," Tom said. The airplane rolled out to walking speed within a hundred feet. I considered it ironic that one of the best landings I would ever see had been judged by one minor flaw.

Today was the day for pilots who loved to land airplanes. A twenty knot crosswind from the north ensured an empty sky, at least in the neighborhood of Davis where the runway lay east-west. The pasture to the north of the airport has a ridge line parallel to the runway. That ridge imparted to a northerly wind a very funny tumble by the time the wind reached the runway. The hangar and the office and the willow tree in the Paille's back yard contributed their disruptions to the wind as well, in the form of roiling eddies and downdrafts.

As I was on my way to my car to go home I saw another airplane in the pattern. Tom called to me and told me to wait, so we could watch the airplane land. The plane started its approach by shortening the downwind leg and turning, too soon I thought, to base. "Watch him now," said Tom. The plane was coming in much too high on base. He was over the end of the runway now, well up.

"He screwed up his approach," I said. "He's too high."

"Just watch," said Tom.

I watched. The airplane turned final after overflying base. He had gone as far as the willow tree, two hundred feet to the north side of the runway. If he came down straight on final he would hit the hangar. But, once he turned, the wind began to push him back. He dipped his right wing and slipped. He lifted the wing, drifted slightly toward the runway, then dipped the wing again and slipped, this time so radically it checked all forward motion. The airplane came down crosscontrolled. For one instant, before I understood what I was watching, I thought for sure he'd crash. Then, he flared the airplane out. The airplane seemed to step from the air to the runway the way a person-steps off an escalator at the end of coming down. No impact. Just walk away. The airplane rolled a few feet and stopped.

"That guy flies for United Airlines," said Tom "He comes out here on-his day off and fools around."

The seventh day of strong north winds. Today we headed west, and when we reached the interstate Tom began showing me a new ground reference maneuver, this one called "Dutch Rolls." He asked me to follow through and watch what he did. He picked out for reference a clover leaf on the interstate two miles south of us, and headed the Cub on a line toward it. Then, he proceeded into a series of aileron moves with the stick - stick left, stick right, stick left, stick right - rhythmically and just swiftly enough that by each time the Cub had rolled into a bank one way the controls had been reversed and it began to roll the other way. Each roll of the Cub was dampened by giving opposite rudder. The effect caused the Cub to sashay through the air, while keeping its heading exact. The cloverleaf stayed steady off the nose. It seemed remarkable. I asked Tom what the purpose was. He explained it was a move to learn as an aid in learning how to slip. It involved the crossing of controls.

When we reached the cloverleaf we turned around and headed back north. Tom gave me the ship to let me try. I started working the stick back and forth. I got my feet tangled up trying to establish the opposite rhythm with the rudder. The airplane broached, and stalled. I hit my forehead on the back of Tom's seat. We recovered. from the stall and reestablished the heading so I could try again. The airplane bucked, gyred around, pitched nose up and yawed. I cursed. I tried again. The airplane jerked, broached again, whipped around slamming me from one wall to the other. For the first time, I became resentful of Tom's ability to fly. It shamed me that he could do this move so naturally and make it seem so graceful.

We broke off and headed west toward Sugar Loaf again. Tom picked out a farm two miles from the base of the mountain. He explained that I would understand Dutch Rolls, or get the hang of how to do them, if I had more feel for the play between the rudder and the ailerons. We were to play a little game, using the farm house as a point of reference. I was to work the rudder but to keep my hands off the stick. Tom was to work the stick but keep his feet off the rudder. The object was to see if he, using ailerons, could make the airplane fly a circle to the right and go around the farm house. I was to oppose his attempts with the rudder, to cross-control the airplane. The experiment became so antic that I forgot my anger entirely. The ailerons produced the turn, albeit in a slip the entire way around, and no action I could take to oppose the turn would stop it. We swapped controls the second time around, and my predicament became Tom's. He could bring us near the stall, but he could not stop the turn.

On the way back to Davis, Tom had me navigate, to see if I could find the airport. To complicate my task, he had me try Dutch Rolls. By slowing the maneuver down, until it felt unnaturally extreme, exaggerating the roll and slowly feeding in the adverse yaw, I could make some semblance of the move Tom asked of me. Finally, I tried one faster, and, entirely inadvertently, I did it. Tom was satisfied with that. He knew, however, and I knew, too, that I didn't know how I did it and dared not press my luck to try for two. I found the airport. That much, at least, showed skill.

When we entered the pattern, I expected Tom to take the controls away. Instead, he asked me to land the airplane. On final approach the crosswind blew us off to the left and I missed the runway.

THURSDAY, APRIL 10TH.

In ground school we continued our review of meteorology. We worked on reading and interpreting area forecasts, terminal forecasts, and the forecasts of winds aloft. Bill Miller came to class tonight. He had the flu and he looked ashen. It crossed my mind that he was going to drop out. I could see by his responses to the questions that Jim asked that he had not read the text, and the chapter on meteorology was the longest in the book. During recess, he took two cigarettes from me. His voice was so hoarse he could hardly speak.

FRIDAY, APRIL 11TH.

I spent the better part of the morning reading VFR Exam-O-Grams, a government publication which was very good on the subject of aviation weather. Some of the advisories were written in the late forties and fifties, and they had about them an old-fashioned, this-will-save-your-life urgency, which made them irresistible to me.

In the afternoon, I drove to National Airport to visit the Washington Flight Service Station. I spent most of my time trying to find a place to park. The station is housed in the General Aviation- building, part of the North Terminal at National. It is the part that most travelers at National never see. The station itself consists of a large office that occupies one corner of the building's main floor.

There in that office, on the walls and on the counter, I found the very charts we had been studying for so long in class. The difference was, of course, that the charts and teletype communiques were live. The pilots here were here for real. Of a sudden, I felt very much out of place. I had joined a line to get at reports that lay in stacks on top of the counter. Real pilots stood before and after me in line. I waited, with my notebook and my pencil in hand, hoping that, if I kept my mouth shut, I could pass. Behind the counter, in the office area, briefers and station personnel were hard at work. They pulled copy from teletype machines. They manned the radio, with its many broadcast points throughout the area. They gave briefings. They answered phones, which seemed to ring incessantly. They were in touch with other airports and with the control tower there. It was one of the busiest flight service stations in the country, and, the closer I drew to the counter, the more fully I realized that this was a professional operation.

When I did get to the counter, I also realized that I did not know which line I had been standing in, or which of the several kinds of reports lay before me on the counter, or for that matter, why I had come to this place. The pilot behind me - who was wearing a blue uniform and a cap and smoked a pipe - made a noise. What did he say? Did he tell me to step aside? I started writing, taking notes. The briefer looked at me suspiciously. I wrote as fast as I could. I don't know what report it was. Why didn't I shave?

The briefer came forward. "Can I help you?" he inquired.

"I'm just getting this information," I replied.

"It's out of date," he said.

* * *

From home I called Tom and cancelled my flying lesson for the afternoon. This was the first time I felt I had to lie to Tom - I told him I was busy - to cover up the fact that I did not want to fly.

MONDAY, APRIL 14TH.

We took the meteorology exam tonight. The exam was disappointing. It was a snap. Nutwell and I compared grades. I beat him by four points. He asked me if I had soloed yet. I asked him if he'd ever done Dutch Rolls. He told me he was thinking about taking a job on the oil pipeline in Alaska. Neither of us believed a word the other said; we are good friends.

Bill Miller was absent from class.

TUESDAY, APRIL 15TH.

The weather was overcast. I called the airport in the morning and spoke with Bill Paille. I told him I did well on my meteorology test. He told me it would rain today, so don't come out.

WEDNESDAY. APRIL 16TH.

The weather today was fair. I showed up at the airport at nine thirty, and Tom and I took off for a review of what I learned so far. Today, I got Dutch Rolls. We worked west of the airport and Tom had me navigate back again. On a clear day I have learned to locate the airport by lining it up between Sugar Loaf to the west and Tridelphia

Reservoir to the east. Damascus, northwest of the airport, provided a landmark closer in. I found that my one innate virtue as a pilot was spotting from the air. My eyesight is not exceptional, but I seem able to pick out anything (except crows). In view of what I had heard, before starting to fly, about the crowded conditions in the airspace above the Eastern Seaboard states, I had been expecting, each day I was up with Tom, to see a number of other small airplanes, as well as larger commercial liners. But that was not the case. There were in fact no large planes to be seen and few small ones. We had seen, perhaps, five. I asked Tom if this were so because most private pilots flew on week-ends. He said that he flew on week-ends, too, in his own plane, and even so, most of the planes he saw were those parked on the ground.

Tom had me fly the pattern back at Davis, then shoot the approach and try to land. I missed the first approach, but, rather than correct for it and try to get the airplane down, I added power and climbed to pattern altitude again. Tom seemed not to approve but didn't countermand the judgement I had shown. I missed the second attempt as well, and once again added power to take the Cub back up. This time Tom had words for me. "I don't want to see you get into the habit of flying missed approaches," he said. "Almost any approach can be recovered, right up until the very end." It was a theme he was to press on me just one time only. The idea registered and stuck.

THURSDAY, APRIL 17TH.

Jim was out of town, so we held no class.

We were beginning a study of the Federal Aviation Regulations, known, according to their initials, as the FAR's. Parts sixty-one and ninety-one of the FAR's concern the student pilot; part sixty-one because it deals with licensure, and part ninety-one because it deals with operating procedures. Part ninety-one is of interest to anyone who flies. The air is far from free.

FAR part ninety-one consists almost entirely of variations on one theme: how to keep airplanes from running into things, especially other airplanes. Aviation has adopted from nautical traditions many practices and rules to govern right-of-way. It has further developed its own practices and rules to govern flight in different kinds of weather: the standards for minimum visibility and clearance from clouds. These standards establish what is VFR, Visual Flight Rules, Marginal VFR, and IFR, Instrument Flight Rules. For most of the flying that Tom and I did, we needed three miles visibility and a clearance of five hundred feet below clouds, one thousand feet above them, and two thousand feet on either side of them.

FRIDAY, APRIL 18TH.

Tom explained that he would show me how to taxi today. It seemed odd to me that I had been flying for several hours but had not learned to taxi, take-off or land. I could appreciate why we had postponed so long on landing and taking off; clearly landings were the most difficult maneuvers of all, and combined parts of all the other maneuvers I had learned. Clearly, taking off was tricky, too. But taxiing, I assumed, was much like driving in a car, perhaps simpler. I eat such assumptions, habitually.

We started off down runway 26, not for the purpose of taking off, but very slowly, hardly faster than a brisk walk. What technique there was was simple: steer with the rudder pedals, which are linked to the tail wheel, and keep the stick back, so the prop. blast would pin the tail to the ground. My goal was to reach the far end of the runway, two thousand feet away. Within a hundred yards from where we started, the little, wobbly tail wheel had castered, like the wobbly wheels on grocery carts, and before I could correct for it the tail swung around to the right and we ran off the runway to the left. We bounced across the grass. The short, stubby stanchions that held the runway lights were placed at intervals along the side of the runway in the grass. The stanchions rose high enough to break an airplane's prop; they were sturdy enough to nose an airplane over should the landing gear roll into one. Tom grabbed the controls away from me and skidded the airplane to a stop. "Try not to hit those runway lights," he said.

He maneuvered the Cub between two stanchions and we circled back across the grass onto the runway again. The tail wheel was linked to the rudder, it is true, but the linkage was two springs, one on either side of a flange controlling the wheel, and those springs lagged somewhat in their responses to the rudder. This placed a premium on the pilot's ability to anticipate a swerve, and so begin correcting before the swerve develops. Furthermore, when we got underway again, and the Cub began to run off the runway to the right, I found the brakes were difficult to reach quickly. The transfer of pressure, from the balls of the feet, which ride the rudder, to the heels, which reach the brakes, was anything but natural. Indeed, it was the opposite of how to work the pedals in a car, and it felt as if I held my feet in stirrups, on a horse.

I stopped the airplane, turned it back onto the runway and resumed my strange ballet. The next time, I almost made it to the end, weaving back and forth from one margin of the runway to the other. But I became overconfident and ran off the pavement into the grass, fifty feet short of the turn off to the taxi strip. Tom coughed. My arm grew weary from holding back the stick. We opened up the door to let in air.

The taxi strip was half the width of the runway, or less, and not paved nearly so well. The grades and humps and ruts were obvious to me. The Cub slowed down on an upgrade. I fed in power but the Cub rolled to a stop. It began to roll backwards. Tom looked out the right and watched the cows. I fed in more power. The Cub stopped and rolled forward again. We went over the top of the grade and down the slope. The Cub picked up speed and got away from me again. Tom picked at something in his teeth. I pulled the power back. The Cub rolled faster. I found one brake but couldn't find the other. The Cub pivoted and ran off the taxi strip to the right. Tom observed the sky.

Throughout the taxiing, my visibility was restricted; I could not see ahead of us. I began to judge our course on the taxi strip, as well as on the runway, by the distance from the left wheel to the margin. If the distance began to close, we were running off to the left. If it began to open, the swerve was to the right. Near the windsock, the taxi strip curved to the left and rejoined the runway. Here, we stopped at the hold-short line to check for traffic in the pattern. From that vantage I could also look out to my left, and see the wheel tracks the Cub left in the grass; many graceful sets of arcs and loops where the Cub's three wheels had run their course, from here down to the western end and back again. "You know," I remarked to Tom, "If you had had me doing this the first day I came out here, there's every chance I'd never have returned the second day."

"I know," said Tom.

We started down the runway the second time. I made it to the end, then couldn't find the brakes in time and overran the runway into the grass. On the taxi strip coming back, I went too fast and ran off three times to the left. "Try one to the right, for variety," said Tom. On the runway for the third time, I ran off to the right. Eventually my legs began to learn, but only when my mind had ceased to think. It seemed there was nothing to think about, that thoughts intruded, took up time, required translation from eye to reflex of the leg and foot. Better to be dumb. My legs began to develop a sense of how much rudder to apply to dampen those growing oscillations from the tail: the swerve one way, the still greater swerve the other way correcting it, the third swerve greater still, and finally running off. My eyes became adept at reading cues. My only thoughts were how to rest my arm. On the taxi strip, at slower speeds, I used both hands to hold the stick, and finally let my right arm hang.

We took a break and started again. The grass of the airport looked like railroad sidings, with so many sets of tracks criss-crossed. Tom introduced a new maneuver. He had me taxi the airplane down the runway at fifteen hundred r.p.m. This was fast enough, as I well knew, to take the airplane off the ground and make it fly. So rather than start with the stick back, as we had been doing, Tom had me put it forward all the way. Then as our rolling speed increased, to forty miles an hour, I was to come back part way with the stick to a neutral position. The technique would cause the tail to be lifted in the air. We would be taxiing on two wheels, on the verge of taking off. At the second of the three turns off to the taxi strip, I was to cut the power and, as the airplane slowed, to ease forward on the stick to keep the tail in air for as long as possible. I would have to steer by the rudder only, since the wheel would be well off the ground.

We gave it a try. I put the stick forward and began opening the throttle. The airplane shot ahead. So much speed startled me after all that work at the slower pace. I eased the stick back. The tail was airborne. The airplane suddenly yawed to the left, then careened off the runway. "Brakes!" yelled Tom. I pulled the stick all the way back, cut the power and jammed the brakes. We skidded between two runway lights and carried on another hundred feet. I was unnerved by that. "Want to quit?" asked Tom.

"No," I said, "I want to try again."

We tried again. The yaw to the left was produced by slipstream rotation, the prop. blast spiraling back and striking the left face of the vertical stabilizer. Since the tail was airborne it was free to weathercock. The yaw was produced by gyroscopic precession as well - the engine changed its plane of rotation when the tail came up and the nose went down. It precessed as a gyroscope and pulled us to the left. "Anticipate," said Tom, "You know it's going to happen."

I knew it was. We went again. I waited. When it happened, I corrected, fast. Right rudder, all the way. But the yaw set in. We started off to left. Then the correction set in. We swerved back to the right, recrossing the runway. I cut the power, hit the brakes. I hauled back on the stick to get the tail down. We skidded and we bounced along the ground.

When the Cub had stopped I asked Tom what went wrong.

"You were an instant late."

"But I got on the rudder as soon as the yaw occurred."

"That's what I mean. That was an instant late."

We taxied back to try again. I checked traffic, entered the runway, turned upwind and stopped. I got my head involved in this.

Anticipation is an act itself; I just can't wait. I put the stick forward. I moved the throttle up. The Cub began to roll. I felt the tail lift off the ground. My right foot drove the rudder bar. The speed picked up. The nose dropped level with the runway now. The tendency to yaw set in. I felt it tug. But the rudder was there ahead of it this time. We stuck, rolling faster by the second taxi turn. "That's good," yelled Tom. I reached to cut the throttle back "No, don't," he yelled. "Add power, now!" I pushed the throttle all the way. The airplane left the runway's centerline and flew.

MONDAY, APRIL 21ST.

We began our class sessions on the FAR's. It was slow going. Bill Miller was absent again tonight.

TUESDAY, APRIL 22ND.

Tom instructed me in the conventional way to fly a take-off in the Cub. We took advantage of the Cub's high Angle of Attack in its normal, three-point taxi roll. Under full power that Angle of Attack would generate the lift necessary to get off the runway. The technique required anticipation of the tendency to veer to the left, and maintenance of the stick in a neutral position. Once we were airborne I let the nose down slightly, so the airplane would accelerate in ground effect. At fifty miles an hour I came back on the stick and we climbed. My first try went so cleanly that Tom congratulated me. Were it not for the fact that I had to fly the airplane up and into the pattern, then come around and try to land, I might have basked all day.

As it turned out, I had ten seconds of the illusion I was good. When we reached a thousand feet, indicated altitude, I rolled into a bank to the left. The torque of the engine assisted me in letting the airplane bank too steeply, however, and my attempt to ride that bank out while climbing brought the airspeed down below fifty. Tom snapped at me. I looked over his left shoulder to scan the instruments. The ball of the slip indicator rolled to the inside. I tried to take off some bank, but I was already on left rudder so the airplane cross controlled. Tom snapped at me again. I told him what I was trying to do. He told me I was wrong.

I neglected to watch our ground references during the turn, and, partly as a result of the sharpness of the turn, I rolled out past my heading. My neat, rectangular course of the pattern was beginning with a warp. The crosswind leg was truncated. The wind, southwesterly today, was now, to us, a quartering headwind from the right. It caused us to drift in the direction of the airport, whose runway should have been perpendicular to the airplane, below and somewhat behind the left wing. The runway appeared on a slight cross angle and just below the left wing tip.

The Cub continued to climb. Tom showed displeasure, now by tapping the altimeter with his index finger. When I looked over his shoulder, I realized we had just passed pattern altitude, which, for the Cubs, was twelve hundred feet at Davis. I divided my attentions to follow two thoughts: to level the airplane, number one; and make the turn to the left, downwind. I tried to do both operations at one time but lacked the security with the controls and the instruments to bring that off. When I pulled the power back to stop the climb, I pulled it back too far. When I had established the bank for the downwind turn I had entered the turn in a climb. Now we lost power, lost airspeed; lost altitude in the middle of the turn, in which the bank once again had rolled up far too steep. I distracted myself with multiple references: out on the right wing I looked at the fairing, which first rose to the horizon, then rose above it. Down the left wing, I looked for the airport. But the wing of course had banked, so it cut off all my view. I tried scanning the instruments all at once, could read them well enough but not interpret the order of corrections to be made. Airspeed, forty five; too low. Altitude, eleven-twenty; falling. Tachometer, nineteen hundred r.p.m.; too low. The needle and the ball showed the bank too steep at forty-five degrees, the ball rolled left to the inside of the turn; showed slip. I relaxed back-pressure but found resistance from the trim. The ship was still trimmed for climbing out, nose high. Rather than follow through against the trim, easily done, I reached around Tom's seat to crank it out. Tom shook his head. I should have added power first. The nose came down. The air speed rose. We lost another fifty feet.

I rolled the airplane out of the turn, having neglected the ground references this time, too. When the left wing rose and the airport reappeared, I realized we had turned by our heading for the second time in a row and now held a course to the east, north-east. Instead of the runway lying parallel to our course, two thousand feet away from us, we closed on it at an angle. Wind drift continued to compound my own errors; the wind quartered now from off our tail from the right.

I re-rolled the Cub through another turn, this time to right. Then, I jumped to the impulse to pull the carb. heat on. In the exchange of grips on the stick, I relaxed back-pressure and the airspeed rose. "Listen to your engine," Tom demanded.

His words brought me up in my seat. The engine was pounding away, overrevved. I pulled the throttle back instead of hauling on the stick. Then, I changed my mind and pulled the stick. The Cub zoomed up. We reached twelve hundred feet again. The airspeed dropped and brought us near the stall. Tom sighed. The airport was falling away, behind us now. We were heading off to the east, south-east, toward Laytonsville. I recorrected with another turn to left.

The point had come to begin the glide. The windsock lay directly off to our left now. I pulled the throttle back with a jerk. Tom snapped at me for abusing the controls. The engine speed fell off to idle and the airspeed dropped to fifty. I reached around Tom and cranked in trim. I let the nose down and we held fifty.

"Okay," said Tom, "Now make your turn." We had glided out over the field east of the airport, and passed over the road from Laytonsville. I looked back to my left at runway 26. The numbers lay below the port side fin of the tail.

I rolled the Cub into a bank to the left. The left wing dropped and blocked my view again. The airplane slipped inside the turn. I over-banked. The stick tugged, as if to beg me to relax the back-pressure. So, I relaxed it. The nose dropped. The airspeed rose. "Hold fifty," said Tom. The wind began to whir through the struts. "Hold fifty," he said again.

We rolled from the turn onto base. The runway reappeared, now ahead of the left wing, below it, and somewhat flatter in perspective. Below the wheel passed a wood shed in a neighboring front yard. "Do you think we will make it in this glide?" Tom asked. I did not wait to think, but stepped up the power to thirteen hundred r.p.m.

We entered the turn to final. We wallowed through the turn, over-banked and slipping, then rolled out to the right of the runway's centerline. The threshold of the runway lay ahead of us three hundred yards, below and to the left of the nose. The wind that had boosted us downwind and on base reduced our groundspeed now. It quartered from ahead and to the left. We drifted to the right. "Correct the drift," said Tom. I crabbed the airplane to the left. "Hold fifty," he said. I pulled the nose up again. The Laytonville road, its telephone lines and trees, swept by beneath the plane. "Align us with the runway," Tom demanded. I crabbed us farther to the left. Furrows of a farm field recrossed in a blur beneath us now. The stand of hardwood trees to the south of the runway no longer appeared below my view but at my level now, and prominent. Turbulence upset the plane. I corrected hastily with ailerons. We wambled as if drunken. Controls were soft, the airplane slow in each response. "Hold fifty," said Tom.

Bushes of the boundary line went by. The top of the hangar lay above my view. Details emerged and moved with speed. "Cut the power," said Tom.

I pulled the throttle back. The numbers of the runway slipped by below the plane.

"Hold fifty."

The runway straightened out ahead of us at last.

"Start coming back."

I pulled on the stick. The nose began to rise.

"Come on back."

I lost the sight of everything ahead.

"Come back!" Tom yelled.

I reacted on the cue, too late. The airport suddenly swelled around the plane. Bam, we hit on the right wheel. "Stick back," yelled Tom. Bam, we came down again on both wheels. "Back! Stick back!" he yelled. I pulled the stick back. The tail weathercocked to right. Bam, we hit again and careened off the runway to the left. The stick bounced. "Stick back!" The stick bounced. The windsock and the runway lights went by. "Brakes!" Brakes. I couldn't find the brakes. Tom grabbed the stick away. He worked the rudder and the brakes. The airplane skidded and we bounced across the grass, skidded on and on and then we stopped. The taxi strip lay before us, off the nose; the runway at our backs.

"Okay," said Tom.

"Okay, what?"

"Okay, we go again."

We taxied ahead to the taxi strip and then around to the hold-short line. I cranked out the trim and turned off the carburetor heat. I checked for traffic and we went again.

The catastrophes accumulated. One landing after another I came in scrambling to line up with the runway, seeing too late each time that the airplane was improperly aligned. Each time we came down, I failed to judge the flare out, and the airplane either hung, ballooned back up, or flew into the runway. When we hit too fast, before the stall had occurred, before I got the tail down or bled the airspeed off or controlled the rotation in the flare, we bounced off the main gears. Each time we bounced I let the stick bounce, too. When the stick bounced, the tail stayed up, depriving us of the Angle of Attack that slowed the plane; depriving us of the tail wheel, which steered, allowing the wind to catch the vertical fin and cause the ship to yaw. Yaw to the left, come down from the bounce yawed. Careen off to the left, veer. Every landing, I ran the airplane off the runway. Each one, I lost control. A dozen tries went by and I became distraught. Each time, Tom wrenched away the controls to salvage the ship from a damaging crash. He kept us front heeling over, ground looping; he wrenched the stick away and jammed the power on to keep us from pancaking from eight feet up. He maneuvered the brakes so our swerves would straighten out and we would thread between instead of hit the runway lights. I came to anticipate the moment in each approach when Tom would grab the stick away, work the rudder, work the brakes, and save the ship. It increased my sense of helplessness, and that, in turn, fed fuel to dread.

At the end of each landing, for the first five, we stopped on the taxi strip to analyze mistakes. But, after five, I had covered all the errors, and on the sixth approach I started through them all again. Finally, Tom said, "Until you set up an approach, hold a constant airspeed and correct for drift, you'll never judge the glide slope. Because the slope will be changing. And each change will change your point of view."

Toward. the end of the morning, my nerves were so shot that I could no longer count on myself for the reflexes I had learned. I let a take-off get away from me and ran off the runway on the take-off roll.

Today was not the first time I had tried to land. Today was the first time I came face to face with it. Landing made me see myself in action. No social dodges could be learned to cover that. I couldn't bluff, exaggerate, equivocate. I could not shift stances, elide from one move to another. Gestures had no part. I could not blame the wind, or the fact that I am left handed.

Tom consoled me with the promise that when I learned to land the Cub, then I would be secure in any other plane. Odd that he insisted several times on using the word when, while I myself was already translating it to if.

* * *

At home I remained preoccupied by flight. In my mind's eye I began reviewing approaches. They played out like film clips, or instant replay on videotape. Each time I came to the flare, the tape ran out.

Later in the day, I concluded that it is the complexity of motion that makes training of the eye so difficult. I picked up on the point

Tom made: that the eye must coordinate perceptions of motions with actions that will change the basis of perception, by altering the attitude and the path of flight. This is so when the airplane enters in the flare. There is rotational movement nose up, which is a change in point of view. There may be yaw and roll to accompany that, and would be in a slip. There is one direction of movement forward, and another direction downward, both blended into one. This blend itself transforms in the flare as the airplane levels out, then stalls and touches down. The eye is used to seeing from head height. It misperceives from higher up and overestimates the height. As the airplane enters in the flare, very suddenly its true motion appears to the eye. The eye recognizes how fast and high the airplane is, but the act of recognition is itself one act too late.

WEDNESDAY, APRIL 23RD.

On the way out to the airport I nearly had a fender-bender, because I was shooting an approach as I drove.

The weather was fair, the wind again was coming from the south. Today, I was intent as I rarely have been intent in all my life. The job was there, in the form of a bottleneck, the flare, which takes from one to three seconds to pass through.

We used runway 26 again today. On the climb to the pattern I did a good job, staying abreast of developments and correcting for the wind. I pulled the throttle back and cranked in trim. We began the downwind glide. "Now watch your turns today," said Tom. "And hold your airspeed." I watched the threshold of the runway recede as the glide carried us out beyond the road from Laytonsville. I made the turn, cutting the leg short. Tom said nothing. He understood my intention. If yesterday we needed power to extend the glide slope, today I would shorten the slope to make the glide itself extend. The wind blew at us from the tail now. The trees beside the road traipsed by beneath the wheel of the Cub. It appeared we had the altitude. I checked the airspeed, checked the position of the runway relative to the wingtip. The slope seemed good to me. I rolled the airplane to the left.

We came around the turn, overbanked and slipping inside the turn. The short turn brought us out to the left of alignment with the runway. In the turn, I had let the nose drop, the airspeed rise. "Hold fifty," said Tom.

We recrossed the road, telephone lines and trees. The perspective of the runway had not flattened yet or foreshortened in my view. I put the Cub in a corrective turn to right.

The airport's boundary shrubs went by. The runway was too deep, too long, for this close in. I dropped the right wing, put the rudder to that left and started the slip. "Wrong way," said Tom.

Wrong way. The wind came from the left. Oh yes, I rolled the Cub the other way, reversed the rudder to the right. The wind shredded around the airfoils jutted out into the flow; the sound seemed rending. The airplane dived. "Control the slip," said Tom. "Hold fifty."

The airspeed rose to sixty-five. The nose of the airplane yawed off to the right. The left wing dropped and aimed down at the ground. The hangar went by. The windsock went by. "Level the wings," said Tom.

I came across with the stick, from the left to the right; took my foot off the rudder. The nose recrossed the runway, right to left; the runway rose to meet us, from the right. Periphery surrounded us and swallowed us inside of it. "Come back!" said Tom.

Come back. Bam! Off the grass to the left of the runway.

"Stick back!"

Stick bounced. Runway lights streaked by underneath the wing struts on the left. Bam, we hit again.

"Stick back!" Tom jerked the controls away from me. He jammed the brakes. He hauled the stick back and held it in its place. The Cub skidded in a straight line, the runway to the right of us the runway lights to left.

We came to a rest. "Number one," said Tom, turning around in his seat to see if I had given up. "Number one," he said again, softening his voice, "You were about two seconds too late recognizing that you had to do a slip to bring down that high approach."

"Okay," I said.

"Number two, you started the slip the wrong way."

I nodded.

"Number three, instead of holding back-pressure in the slip, you relaxed back-pressure and the airplane dived."

I nodded, put in a little throttle and the Cub rolled ahead over the grass onto the turn-off to the taxi strip

"Furthermore," said Tom, "If you're going to slip, you have to gauge your alignment by sighting off the low wing."

The Cub swung around to the left onto the taxi strip.

"Otherwise," Tom continued, "Too much aileron for the amount of opposite rudder, so the airplane ended up turning after all, in spite of the wind."

We bumped along, went up the grade and over the top. Tom let the door down. The wind came in.

"And, if you've relaxed back-pressure," he said, "With the exaggerated amount of slip you put in, then the rate of descent becomes so great that momentum carries the ship right through ground effect. You hit without the flare."

Down the slope of the grade I pulled the throttle back to idle. The Cub coasted along, pleasantly jostling.

"So number four, you've got to come out of the slip earlier; at least reduce it, so you can control the flare. Number five, you missed the runway."

I put the brakes on. The Cub pulled up short, by the windsock. I looked past Tom to check for traffic coming in.

"Number six, you didn't hold the stick back after the first touch-down; so when we bounced you lost control. And seven, you aren't using your eyes properly to look out in the flare. You should be looking well ahead of the airplane and off to one side of the nose."

I nodded my assent to this.

"Where do you look when we enter the flare?" Tom asked.

"Straight ahead."

"And what do you see?"

"The nose or the airplane blocking my view." I pushed the carb. heat off and cranked out trim. The Cub rolled onto the runway and swung around to the left in alignment. Tom pulled the door shut and we took off.

In the climb-out he yelled back to me. "The idea of cutting short the approach didn't work."

"I know," I yelled. "We came in high."

"So what are you going to do?" he asked.

I trimmed the Cub for the remainder of the climb and put us through the turn to the cross wind leg. We reached pattern altitude and I levelled out. I cranked out the trim and made the turn downwind. "Extend the downwind leg," I said. He nodded his approval. I put the carb. heat on again and corrected for the drift. "You forgot one thing," I yelled.

Tom leaned back. "What's that?"

"I overbanked my turn from base."

"'You overbank them all," he said.

I pulled the throttle back. We began the glide downwind. I cranked in trim again. I carried the glide out beyond the road and over the neighboring yard as far as the woodshed, then slipped inside the turn to base. I came back on the stick and kept the nose up, holding fifty throughout the turn. We coursed along base. I estimated the height; it seemed the same to me. I estimated the timing of the turn to final; it seemed the same as well. We slipped inside the turn. The wing blocked my view. When we rolled out we were to the left of the runway.

But now the slope looked right; the glide at least was true. I held heading in alignment with the runway. The crosswind blew us to the right. We came back across the road and the furrows of the field. The touchdown would be in the first third of the runway. The sense of that emerged clearly. The alignment was going to true in time, because of drift.

"Okay," said Tom, "Start coming back."

We crossed the hedges of the boundary line. Airspeed fifty. Tom turned around in his seat and looked at me. "Don't look at the airspeed," he snapped, "Look at the airport!" The numbers of the runway whisked by beneath the plane. Turbulence hit us. I came back on the stick. I looked out, far and to the left but could not tell whatever it was I saw. Slopes, lawns, runway lights, fences, airplanes parked in rows. I came back on the stick and we entered the flare. With a whoosh the runway went whizzing by beneath us; distance, midground, foreground blur. I failed to fix on any one thing.

"Power!" yelled Tom.

The stick was back, in final rotation.

"Power!"

I shoved the power on. The Cub came down from pancake height and wham! Off the runway, main gear bounce. Teeth jarred.

"Cut the power! Stick back!"

I cut the power. The stick had bounced from me again. Bam, we hit again. Kaboom, the third time down and off the runway over the grass to grandmother's house we go.

* * *

I want to quit.

THURSDAY, APRIL 24TH.

In ground school, Nutwell caught up to me at recess. "How many hours have you got?" he said.

"Oh, eighteen or so."

"And you haven't soloed yet? Tsk. Tsk."

I retreated from George and took up refuge with Bill Miller. I confided to him that I had no idea how to land the Piper Cub. He pooh-poohed the idea. "Once your eye begins to get the hang of looking out the side and judging height, it'll all come together...." and he snapped his fingers " ...just like that."

FRIDAY, APRIL 25TH.

By mutual consent, Tom and I passed by the lesson for today. In the mail, my medical certificate arrived. The FAA decided I was fit.

MONDAY, APRIL 28TH.

We continued studying the FAR's. Bill Miller was absent tonight. I avoided Nutwell.

TUESDAY, APRIL 29TH.

It rained. I spent the day studying the FAR's. Home movies continued to play inside my head. The feature film was runway 26.

WEDNESDAY, APRIL 30TH.

The rains came down all day. Each day away from the airport, my wounds healed.

Tonight, we had a special session in school to make up for the day we lost two weeks before. We took the test on the FAR's. Bill Miller did not come; he had dropped out of class.

THURSDAY, MAY 1ST.

We began the Airman's Information Manual, popularly known as the AIM.

FRIDAY, MAY 2ND.

I showed up at the airport in mid afternoon, the first clear day all week. The air was still.

Tom and Bill were working in the hangar. "Long time no see," said Tom. My mood was contagious, so we exchanged few words after that.

I checked out the Cub. Tom came out and we went through the start-up. Runway 26 was active. Tom pulled the door closed. I checked for traffic. We rolled out onto the runway and took off.

On the first approach, when we came down final, the seat cushion worked loose. I had fidgeted too much, trying to get a view of the runway out ahead. I tried to fidget with my hips to get the cushion back. The more I squirmed, the more it wedged, forward of the seat frame now, between the backs of my thighs and the front edge of the seat. That kind of comic desperation was killing me. I wanted to scream, rage. I had no room against the seat belt and the stick to move, and sat up on the wedge of the cushion and front bar of the seat, to see the numbers of the runway scoot past. The runway flattened out. I pulled the stick back and flared. We touched down and rolled out half way down the runway to a stop.

I turned off onto the taxi strip, unloosened my seat belt and jammed the cushion back in place. "What did, you do right?" asked Tom, scratching his head..

"I haven't the faintest idea," I replied.

We went around again. I set up for the second approach. On final, I misjudged the slope and then the flare and flew the airplane into the runway. We bounced catastrophically. The tail stayed up. We came down the second time and continued bouncing in kangaroo hops for the next five hundred yards. "What did you do wrong?" asked Tom, when we stopped.

"I still don't know," I answered. "I did the same thing as before."

We taxied back and went around again. On final, Tom asked how the slope was. I told him it was fine. We landed long, I had to slip. Before we got the airplane down and stopped, I overran the runway and skidded through the grass. Some thirty feet ahead stood the wooden boundary fence.

We went around again. I came in short, lost my alignment with the runway, added power, scrambled with the stick and rudder to get the airplane back in line. One corrective turn after another at low speed, low altitude. The Cub gave out and stalled. I bounced it on. The stick jarred loose from my grasp. We ended in the grass.

I neared the end of my tether. Tom neared his as well. He railed at me. I railed back. "Why can't I land the airplane, Tom?"

"I wish I knew," he shouted. "But I know this. You cannot bring this airplane in eight feet above the runway, near a stall, and then fly slaloms back and forth."

The next time down I flew a missed approach.

Having regained pattern altitude, we flew the pattern once again. On the final leg this time, I misperceived the flare and misaligned the track as well. I scrambled to the left. We touched down sidling. The Cub heeled and nearly hit the wingtip on the ground. I felt I could go no farther. But we taxied back and went around again. I bounced, ran off to the left. Once more. We landed long, ballooned back up and bounced.

I kept well hidden from Tom's face; the only advantage to sitting behind him in that ship. Each bummer took some part of me. I recognized how near I was to tears. I wanted to get out of the airplane. I wanted to tell Tom, "That's it." I wanted to go over and get in my car. I wanted to drive away. I could still go to ground school (where I was an A student and very bright) and not tell them (who are "they?" "them"?) a thing. Ah, yes. But I kept holding the carrot stick in front of me, hanging on with a failure that ran on hope.

"You want to go around again?" asked Tom.

"I do."

* * *

Nearly forty-eight hours went by before I spoke my mind to Gloria. Sunday afternoon I told her how I felt. I even mentioned the episode with the seat cushion. I asked her if she thought I ought to quit. She shook her head. "I think you ought to sit on the edge of your seat," she said. "It was the only thing you tried so far that worked."

MONDAY, MAY 5TH.

We took our ground school test on the AIM. I have a beggar's pride. I scored a ninety-six.

MONDAY, MAY 6TH.

The comeback from the bottom doesn't have to begin. One can sink forever. That thought chilled me as I pulled into the airport's drive. I'm old; not <u>that</u> old.

I checked out the Cub. When I was ready, I called Tom. We nodded, grunted, a manner of hello.

I climbed in. He did the duty with the prop. Brakes on. Stick back. Throttle closed. "Switch off," said Tom.

"Switch off." I primed the engine twice.

He pulled it through. "On both," he said.

"Contact."

He pulled it through again. The engine started. The oil pressure rose. Tom climbed aboard. I pulled the door shut.

I ran the engine up. Left mag. Right mag. Carb. heat. I pulled it back to idle, worked the flight controls. I checked the time, three minutes past ten. I checked the windsock, the wind northwest, ten to fifteen miles per hour, gusting. Runway twenty six was active. I set the altimeter. The day was fair.

The Cub rolled out and turned to the runway. The pattern was clear. We rolled ahead and onto the runway. I swung the ship around to the right and moved the throttle up to full.

On the climb-out I crabbed over to the right to compensate for drift. Below us, I saw laundry lines strung in the backs of suburban lots. Bed sheets and T shirts flapped in the wind.

We turned cross wind. At twelve hundred feet I levelled out. We turned downwind and started on the run. To myself I made two alternating notes: Stick back. Get up in the seat. Stick back. Get up in the seat.

I pulled the power off and cranked in trim. We started in the glide. The Cub passed over the Laytonsville Road and I cut the downwind leg short there. I watched the fairing on the right wing rise, and stopped it when it reached horizon height. Stick back. Get up in the seat. The airspeed held, fifty through the turn. The Cub rolled out on base.

The runway, on a perpendicular to us, lapsed from the port quarter to the beam. I rolled into the turn to final, keeping the fairing even for the second time on the line of the horizon. The low wing, for once, did not obstruct my view. Hold fifty. Stick back. Get up on the edge of the seat.

We came out on final, our ground speed reduced. The wind quartered from ahead and to the right, its effects rendering the glide slope steep. The road went by below. I made my move to get up on the edge of my seat.

Once up out of the bucket, my new position added three inches to my height in the cockpit. The Cub flew over the airport's boundary now. I straightened my back and added two more inches. We crossed the numbers of the runway. I tilted my head to the left. An entire new world opened up. I saw as if first born. Twenty degrees of azimuth enlarged the compass of my sight. I saw details in the foreground, objects in the midground, contours in the distance, line and shape, depth and height; around the hood, below the engine cowl ahead, aside, the runway lights, perspective, lines of taxi turns, slopes and cants of land.

The Cub flared out. The nose rode up. I played the stick, hefting it. We schussed above the runway in the flare. Two seconds passed. We settled down and puttered on the roll out. All done. Stopped and turned off to the taxi strip. An easy thing, a toy. Two seconds in the flare was so much time; for once, I only needed one. It meant my solo was in sight.

WEDNESDAY, MAY 7TH.

The wind changed overnight. It came from the northeast this morning. We were using runway 08.

Today, I had to learn to slip the airplane all the way down final and into the flare; to land with one wing low, the left wing, and opposite rudder to the right. On one approach, I picked up the technique Tom had spoken of, to sight the point of touchdown off the low wing in the slip. It was the one point in the runway that seemed to come straight at us as we slipped. Points beyond it seemed to rise. Points in front all seemed to sink. Points to left or right spread farther left or right. It means I held a constant airspeed in the slip, controlled the slip and so controlled the track. Tom was pleased. At the end of the session, a dozen landings, he told me he liked the way I handled the crosswind today. "If you do this well on Friday," he remarked, "I'll let you try it solo."

* * *

Wednesday night I could not sleep. "Every time I thought about soloing the Cub, my heart rate pumped back up again, and I lay there, the drum beating furiously inside my breast.

THURSDAY, MAY 8TH.

I felt I had an appointment with the dentist. It did no good to realize that things went on happening beyond my control, daily in my life. It was the thought that I might expose just how little control I had on them.

It is a dictum in aviation that a student's first solo provides a watershed. Jim once remarked in class that he had known no happier day all his years of flying than the day of his first solo. The commercial students echoed Jim in that.

In class it occurred to me that I did not even know what we were studying anymore. I also felt a need to confide what I was about to do tomorrow to someone in the class. It was as if to leave a legacy (in case I didn't come back?). I felt I must be circumspect in my choice, so I picked Joe Earhle. Joe told me I'd do fine. Anyone would have said the same, but the remark, when it came from Joe, seemed to have more weight. Joe was a friend, for sure, but he was a dentist too.

FRIDAY, MAY 9TH.

I slept well, but it was on my mind, the moment I awoke.

Gloria told me she would send me good vibrations, at the appointed hour. The appointed hour was three o'clock.

How many times did I tie my shoe laces today? How many times did I tuck in my shirt, check the weather, check to see if my belt was pulled a notch tighter than was usual? Why did lunch taste so good, so memorable, each bite? I believe Leif Erikson set out this day. I'm certain today was Schubert's birth.

I was drawn, magnetized by the airport. I arrived at quarter after one. Tom was having lunch on the lawn outside. He was in the company of a woman friend. He made introductions. Paula, his friend, invited me to share their lunch. I declined the invitation, and thanked her just the same. Tom took note that I was there two hours early for our flight.

I went by myself to be alone with the Cub. I checked the airplane out with an attentiveness to every nut and bolt and cotter pin that was remarkable, even for me. I rolled the Cub over to the grass and sat on the wheel, absorbed in my thoughts, while I stared at the windsock and T.

The sky was overcast today, but the ceiling was ten thousand feet above the ground. Our area lay below two stationary fronts. The weather was ideal for landing an airplane. The wind was very gentle from the east. Runway 08 was active. I liked that runway more than runway 26, in spite of having only one day's practice using it. The approach end of runway 08 presented itself more openly to view from the air. The airport's boundary fence, seen from the air on final, seemed to square off the threshold of the runway. The lay of the airport gave a crest to the runway, which made a natural aiming point for the touchdown or the flare.

Tom came down. "Well, you've got a perfect day," he said.

"Yes I do," I agreed, and we set out on our routine.

A moment later, we had taken off, and a moment after that Tom pulled the throttle closed. We were still on the climb-out, still within the pattern. "What's up?" I shouted.

"Your engine just quit," he said. He was holding the throttle closed; I couldn't have opened it, even with force. I had no choice. I put the nose down and picked a field. We came down over the field's fence and flared out. Tom put the power on again and yelled climb. I came back on the stick. The Cub climbed out.

A moment later, he pulled the throttle closed again. We repeated the process. Each time, I picked out a field upwind, when possible, of our position. I established a glide, then tracked down to the field for the emergency approach. Once, I overestimated how far we could glide. We came in short. Instinctively, I reached for the power. Tom held it off. "Too dam bad," he yelled. We were going to set down on the fence when Tom opened the throttle, and the ship scooted over the top, our landing gear clearing the fence rail by a yard. "You see?" he yelled, as we climbed again.

"I see," I said, as perspiration creamed my forehead. Throughout the maneuvers, Tom explained the points to me. Better high than short; you can always slip. All fields look relatively clean from the air, but from up close they look stubbly, rock-strewn, lined with ditches, furrows, pocked with holes. Pick one and stick to it, don't change your mind at the end. Defer to last resort a forced landing on a road; powerlines and trees that overhang can do you in. Land upwind if possible. Always keep an eye out for landing spots in normal flight, as a part of the routine in flying, as much so as scanning the instruments. The surprise that accompanies an engine failure makes it all the more difficult to select a landing site. Get the nose down, establish the glide immediately. If you have to land on furrowed ground, land with the line of furrows, and not across the grain. An airplane coming in dead stick makes a very lonely sound, like the wind in the willows.

I was hot today. Tom picked out a field and had me fly rectangular courses. I flew them to the left, squared off the turns neat as a pin; flew them to the right and did as well. It pleased him. We flew northwest and found the house where Ovill's parents lived. Tom had me fly turns-about-a-point around a tree in their back yard. "They don't mind," said Tom, "We do it all the time."

On the way back to Davis, he asked for Dutch Rolls. I sashayed the Cub through a dozen rolls and kept the nose steady on a point. "You're on today," said Tom.

"I know," I said, and realized that brought me to the moment that much sooner.

In the pattern, Tom cut the power midway into the downwind leg. He couldn't have picked a worse spot. Had it been sooner, I could have landed downwind; just hitched over to the left and dropped the airplane on. Had it been later, we could have made it in a routinely shortened glide. But, midway down the leg we had half the runway ahead and half the runway behind. I flew on as far as the end of the runway, then brought the Cub around to the left in a long arc. We rolled out of the turn with half the runway gone, but all the altitude was gone as well. I flared and dropped us on. We rolled out long. "Not bad," said Tom, "A little sloppy, but you learned."

We took off and went around again. This time, Tom cut the power a little sooner. He was splitting hairs with me. He was looking for that point that is precisely no man's land. I felt that this was it. Tom laughed. I came around the same wide arc, but this time we had less runway by two hundred feet and more altitude to kill before we got to it. Since the Cub was in a bank to the left, I jammed right rudder. Then I played the rudder, more and less, more and less, adjusting the slip to continue the turn, the way we had done when we flew around the farm the day Tom taught me to do Dutch Rolls. We turned, we came around and dropped, nose yawed, until the flare. I rolled the ship to even keel again and stalled it on. "It's crude but it's all right," said Tom.

On the turn off to the taxi strip, I stopped. No words, no signs had told me to, but the moment seemed to seize on us. Tom knew and I knew, and neither of us had to say it to the other. He turned around in his seat and looked directly into my eyes. I looked directly, back in his. His face was blushing. I felt my face was blushing, too. "Do you think you can make it around on your own?" he asked.

"I believe I can," I answered.

He asked for my log book. I gave it to him. While he wrote, I taxied the Cub back to the western end of the taxi strip. Tom handed me the book when we stopped. I read his entry: "Review. Emergencies. Take-offs and landings. OK for solo." Signed: Thomas E. Young. "Remember," he said, "The Cub will get off fast now that I'm gone, and it will glide flat."

I nodded that I understood. Tom unlatched the door and climbed out. He looked back in. "I'll be watching," he said, "I'll be right here."

I nodded again. He shut the door. I latched it closed. For the next two seconds, I surveyed my domain, my airplane now. The cabin seemed, for some reason, large.

I cranked the trim out and turned the carburetor heat off. There were so many things to do, I could occupy my mind with the sequence of items, one by one, and never pause to let ulterior notions dwell. I checked for incoming traffic. The Cub sounded very light on the gravel as it rolled ahead to runway 08. On the runway, it felt very light as it swung around into alignment.

I put the power on. The Cub started rolling. I held the stick neutral. In almost no time, the ship and I were off. I looked down at the gas pumps and the hangar to the left. Just the trace of a thought passed by: it's too late now, I'm airborne.

The Cub reached four hundred feet very swiftly, effortlessly it seemed, and I rolled into the turn to the cross-wind leg. The ship reached twelve hundred feet before the turn to downwind came. I trimmed it out in cruise, then made the turn. No sooner was I up, time came to think of the approach. I put the carb. heat on, corrected the track. The runway lay out to the left a good distance. I could see Tom, standing by the corner of the runway at the approach end. He was looking up at me.

I could hear his voice, "Hold fifty. Hold fifty," in its echoes in my mind. I pulled the power back. The Cub began to glide. I cranked in trim. I made a note, to get up on the edge of the seat on final. I made a note, to keep the stick back, after touching down, I made the turn to base.

The glide was flat. I had taken the downwind leg a little beyond the normal turning point. On base, I still had altitude. It would pay off in time to make an early flare. I made the turn to final. The Cub came out of the turn true before the runway. This was the best approach turn I had ever flown. The slope was true. I would hit the flare at the crest of runway 08. I saw Tom. His hands were on his hips.

I looked out ahead at the runway, and I saw another airplane coming in to land the other way. We were landing head on. He was in his approach almost at the threshold of runway 26.

I put the power on. To full. I rolled the Cub to right and came back on the stick. The Cub climbed out. I rolled it to the left again, climbed hard. From the window, I saw the other airplane - blue and white - flare out. I motioned in the window to Tom. Tom had swiveled, watching me. He watched me now, his hands still on his hips. When he saw me point down the runway, he turned around in time to see the other airplane land.

I climbed on back to pattern altitude again. I retrimmed the Cub and reflew the whole circuit. I kept my mind off the episode below. I was so charged up and high it did not matter to me now. I flew the second glide, brought the Cub in low over the fence, flared out in the first quarter of the runway and dropped it on.

When I turned off to the taxi strip, I saw Tom, running my way. I stopped and let the door down. He stuck his head inside the cockpit. "You okay?" he asked.

"I'm fine," I said.

Tom's face was taut. I had never seen him in a rage before. "You're doing great," he said, "Go do two more." Then off he ran, toward the blue and white plane.

I shut the door and taxied on. I cranked out trim, pushed off the carburetor heat, checked traffic in the pattern and took off. In the climb-out, I could see the airplane clearly, parked beside the gas pumps in the service area. The pilot was nowhere to be seen, nor was Tom. The man had landed with no pattern, a straight-in approach, down wind and down T.

The second time around, I greased it on.

I taxied back and went again. The third time down I was too confident. I pulled the flare too soon and bounced. At the end of the roll out, I pulled off the runway to the left and taxied the Cub directly to its berth. Mina came out from the office. I shut the engine down. Tom was not there. I climbed out of the airplane and noticed it was Spring. Flowers had bloomed. Grass had grown up, and weeds. Trees were in leaf. Mina was beaming. I had never seen her smile before. "Tom's just so happy for you," she said. "You did just fine."

Mina stayed with me and helped me tie the airplane down. She helped me gas it up. When we started for the office, the pilot of the blue and white plane came out. He dropped his gaze, avoiding mine. At the door of the office I met Tom. He shook my hand. He was as happy, every bit, as I was.

Inside the office sat Bill Paille, the wise old man. "Well, what do you think?" I asked Bill while extending my hand to shake his.

"I think it was a miracle," said Bill.

III

MONDAY, MAY 12TH

Fame so fleet. I was exuberant all week-end. In class again, I decided
I had to tell people. I raised my hand. Jim called on me. I said I was
involved in an <u>incident</u>.

"An incident?" he asked. "You mean your engine quit?"

"No," I said. "Friday I took my first solo, and on the very first
time down there was another airplane landing the opposite direction
on the same runway."

"What did you do?" asked Jim.

"I put the power on and flew around," I said.

"That's not an incident," he said. "That's a commonplace."

* * *

We had begun the study of navigation in class, and our introduction to the subject dealt with the use of the computer and the plotter. The computer was a small, circular slide rule whose scales are
calibrated to solve the routine problems of navigation. Such problems include conversions, such as nautical miles to statutory miles (1
nautical mile equals 1.15 statutory miles), knots to miles per hour,
Celsius (or Centigrade) to Fahrenheit, indicated altitude to pressure
altitude, pressure altitude to density altitude, indicated airspeed to
true airspeed; plus simple equations to solve for speed, time or distance; fuel quantities, fuel rates of consumption, or time. On the back

of the computer there is a wind grid to solve problems of drift, heading and ground speed. The computer is small in order to fit in one hand, ostensibly to be used by the pilot in flight.

The plotter is a straight edge ruler, *cum* compass protractor, whose scales conform to the scales of sectional and world aeronautical charts.

TUESDAY, MAY 13TH.

I took the day off. I felt like basking. I called Tom and put the request to him in just those terms. "What do I care?" he replied.

WEDNESDAY, MAY 14TH.

Today, I got down from my high horse and went out to the airport. When I pulled into the parking lot I realized that what I had been mistaking for sheer exuberance was also my relief. The sight of the airplane still filled me with dread.

THURSDAY, MAY 15TH.

In school, we took the test covering the use of the computer and the plotter.

FRIDAY, MAY 16TH.

Today was a warm day and a fair one, the first truly warm day since I began. Tom put me in the second Cub today, one I had used before on one occasion while flying with him. Today, he sent me off solo from the very start. He wanted me to build up my time with landings.

MONDAY, MAY 19TH.

No class. Jim was out of town.

TUESDAY, MAY 20TH,

A sunny day today but the wind was unstable from the south. Tom sent me out solo to practice takeoffs and landings. I had to get over the notion that I needed to be red hot in order to be competent. Tom understood that. Cold competence had its part to play too, which was most of the time.

WEDNESDAY, MAY 21ST.

The sun was bright again today, and by mid-morning the day was warm. I had become so resigned to practicing takeoffs and landings in the Cub that, like the repeat offender who gets used to the jail, I found I could look forward to it.

In the office afterwards, Tom announced my first cross-country flight. We would go Friday, weather permitting, to Bay Bridge Airport, some forty-seven miles to the east, southeast of Davis.

THURSDAY, MAY 22ND.

We proceeded with our study of navigation in class. We were working on charts now, and dead reckoning. Of the several charts available to the private pilot, the sectional chart, or "sectional" as it is known, is the one used commonly. Sectional charts are published twice a year by the Department of Commerce. They are compiled by the National Oceanic and Atmospheric Administration and National Ocean Survey, with advice from the Department of Defense. The scale of the chart is one inch to eight miles.

Washington Sectional covers an area that begins, in its southwest corner, with Durham, North Carolina, and extends eastward into the Atlantic. The chart includes the coast line as far north as Asbury Park, New Jersey. It runs west into Pennsylvania, taking in Philadelphia and cutting through Harrisburg, and extending on, well into the Appalachian Highlands.

One of the problems we had in class was that of discriminating between true and magnetic courses and headings. Now that we had charts before us, the problem seemed simpler. True courses and true headings refer to the geographical north pole, which is also the reference for the chart. Magnetic courses and magnetic headings refer to the magnetic north pole, where lines of magnetic force about the earth converge. Since the compass is the only direction-seeking instrument on most planes, and since the compass points to magnetic north, it follows that some allowance must be made if the pilot wishes to track a true course from a magnetic heading. That allowance is called variation. In Washington, where magnetic north lies eight degrees west of true north, the variation of eight degrees must be added to the true course to derive a magnetic course, or added to the true heading to derive a magnetic heading.

A third set of terms, compass course and compass heading incorporates the principle of deviation. Deviation occurs when a compass needle deflects from magnetic north because of small magnetic disturbances inside the airplane Most of these disturbances are the result of the radio, the amount of steel in the airplane, and the magnetic field around the induction coil in the airplane's ignition. Deviation differs for each compass in each airplane, and usually differs from one heading to another. But it can be measured and the amount of deviation for the various headings is posted on a "deviation card" placed below the compass in the plane.

Dead reckoning is an estimate of a compass heading that will keep a plane on a true course from one point to another. The pilot usually begins the process of dead reckoning by drawing the true course on the chart. Typically, the course would be a straight line from the point of departure to the point of arrival, though, in the case of longer or more complicated courses, the course can be broken up into legs or segments. My course from Davis Airport to Bay Bridge would be 113 degrees from true north, a straight line 47 statutory miles in length, according to scale.

The next step involves a weather briefing in order to determine the strength and direction of the winds aloft, at the altitude the pilot plans to fly, in the vicinity covered by the course, and for the time the flight would take place. Such a briefing is usually obtained near to flight time, to improve the chances that the forecast will be accurate.

The procedure for converting a true course to a true heading requires vector analysis. We learned it the old-fashioned way in class by breaking components of motion down into diagrams of a wind triangle. Then, we learned it the faster way, using the wind grids of our computers. In either case, the effects of wind on the course of the airplane and on its ground speed are established. The true heading is the way the airplane must point when it flies in order to correct for drift. The angle between the true heading and the true course is called the wind correction angle.

The next step is to convert the true heading to a magnetic heading. In my case, it would be to add eight degrees. The final step would be to add or subtract the degrees of deviation for that heading, and so convert the magnetic heading to a compass heading. It would be the compass heading that the pilot will adhere to in the flight.

One other estimation is involved in dead reckoning, and that is an estimation of ground speed. If there is a component of headwind present, the pilot subtracts it from the true airspeed, and the difference is the ground speed. If there is a component of tailwind present, the pilot adds that to the true airspeed, and the sum will be the ground speed. Once the ground speed is predictable, then the *en route* time for the flight is predictable, and so, too, the arrival time. Other omputations concerning fuel, or the time between checkpoints along the route, then figure in, until the pilot has an entire navigational log worked out before the plane leaves the ground.

FRIDAY, MAY 24TH.

I spent the morning preparing for that afternoon's flight. The study of an air chart includes somewhat more than a study of representative terrain. The chart includes man's impositions on the air space as well. The FAA and Department of Defense have devised elaborate boundaries, placing degrees of restriction on various kinds of flights. The Eastern Seaboard is especially notorious for such controlled air space. My course was to thread between a Terminal Control Area, which surrounds Washington National Airport and Andrew's Air Force Base, and an Airport Traffic Area, which surrounds Baltimore Washington International Airport. The Terminal Control Area is a huge, three dimensional design reaching seven thousand feet above the ground and it is shaped like an upside-down wedding cake. To fly into that space was taboo for me. Tom and I would have to sneak under the edge of the outermost tier. The Airport Traffic Area would also be taboo. It reaches five miles out from the center of the airport and extends three thousand feet above the ground. We would miss the southern circumstance of it, if we stayed on course, by half a mile. That whole corridor, between Washington and Baltimore, is a region saturated with commercial air traffic, and the area to the east of it, near the bay, is a corridor for military jets from several coastal bases. My mind filled with the image of a never-ending string of Boeing 727s cutting across our path.

So far, I had done my preflight planning according to the book. I was fastidious about it. I wanted to know if the book came true. After lunch, I drove to the National Airport, to revisit the Washington Flight Service Station. It was time to get the weather briefing. The book recommended that a pilot go in person, as opposed to calling on the phone. I thought, if the briefer can see me scratching my head, maybe it would help.

I arrived at National with my clipboard full of toys, utensils for a cross-country trip: checklist, log book, medical certificate, FCC operator permit, Maryland pilot's registration, chart, plotter, computer, navigation log. In my pocket I had scratch sheets, notebook, pencils; in my wallet twenty dollars to buy gas. Were it to be a longer trip, I would have packed my lunch.

Washington Flight Service Station on a Friday afternoon is busier than at any other time of the week. Washington is a flight-minded town. I felt I had two advantages this time over my earlier visit: first, that I had been there before, and second, that I knew what I was looking for. Neither counted for much. By the time I stood in line and reached the counter where the reports lay, I had ahead of me the larger chore of interpreting them. There were scores of reporting points for the winds aloft forecasts, and each reporting point was codified on the teletype print-out by a three letter identifier. I figured Baltimore would be listed as "BAL." I didn't find it and I took my time looking. "Help you?" asked the briefer.

"Yes, please," I replied. "Winds aloft at Baltimore."

"Winds aloft at Westminster," he said.

I thought he was asking me, so I repeated myself. "At Baltimore," I said.

"Westminster," he replied.

"Okay, Westminster," I conceded.

"EMI," he said.

"EMI," I said, like a parrot learning French.

He pointed to the teletype report. EMI lay below his fingertip. "Two-forty at fourteen; two-sixty at eighteen," he said.

I scribbled it down. He looked at me and I at him. "Where is EMI?" I asked.

"Near Baltimore," he said.

"What's Baltimore's forecast for this afternoon?"

"Scattered, four thousand; broken, eight thousand; five miles in smoke and haze," he said, without even so much as glancing at the sheet.

I was on my way. I arrived at Davis early. Tom was gone, off flying with another student. I needed the time to complete my navigation log, so I spread my materials on the table in the office. Mina was there at work on the books. Neither of us said so much as a word of hello. Mina worked perfunctorily and routinely. I worked in a dither and drank Cokes. The forecast, two-forty at fourteen, meant the wind would be coming from two hundred forty degrees, true, at fourteen knots, at an altitude of three thousand feet. At six thousand feet it would be from two hundred sixty degrees, true, at a speed of eighteen knots. The lower altitude would apply to me, and my first step was to convert the wind speed from knots to miles per hour, roughly sixteen.

The next step was to determine the true heading, for which I needed the true airspeed at the altitude I planned to fly, three thousand five hundred feet. Since Tom and his student had taken the second Cub, the Cub he and I were to fly was tied down in the berth. I bolted out the door and ran over to the Cub. I opened the door and reached in to set the altimeter to station elevation. The barometric pressure showed up in the Kollsman window at the bottom of the instrument. We had a station pressure of 30.13 inches of mercury, which was roughly two-tenths of an inch above a standard pressure, 29.92 inches, for mean sea level. I rushed back to the office and let the office door slam behind me. Mina looked up. We said hello.

True airspeed worked out to seventy miles per hour (indicated airspeed sixty-five). I turned the computer over and worked the wind grid to solve for drift. The solution showed a tailwind component of nine miles an hour and a crosswind component, from the right, of thirteen. The wind correction angle would be eleven degrees to the right of the true course. Our true heading, therefore, was 124 degrees. The tailwind would produce a ground speed of seventy-nine miles per hour.

I added variation and got a magnetic heading of 132 degrees. When I was at the Cub I could have noted the deviation numbers for the general direction we would be flying, but I overlooked it in my rush. Now I bolted out again and ran over to the Cub. The card read, "'For 120 degrees, steer 120," which meant there was no compass deviation on that heading. I noted the fact and ran back. When I huffed into the office, Mina was waiting for me. "For Cristsakes slow down," she scolded. I closed the door behind me slowly, then bought another Coke.

I had spent six hours studying the chart and developing a navigation log for a flight whose *en route* time solved out at thirty-six minutes. Tom arrived with his student. I sat back with satisfaction as Tom reviewed my plans. In four minutes time, he had rechecked all my work. He mentioned he felt wary about flying so close to Baltimore's air space. "We'll be legal," I said.

"Who wants to be legally dead?" he replied.

In spite of our disagreement, Tom determined that I should have my way. We took off at ten past three. During the climb-out, I noted the time and wrote the figure down on my navigation log. The log was clipped to my clipboard. I put that aside, between the seat and wall of the cockpit. I folded the chart open to a rectangular area that covered our course, and put the chart away in the pocket on the seat-back in front of me. I thought I had the course memorized, and all the check points well in mind. I thought I had the entire navigation log in mind. The procedure for dead reckoning allowed an extra five minutes to the *en route* time to take off and climb to altitude, plus another five minutes at the end, for the descent and approach to the destination. I expected this trip to be by the book.

As we left the pattern, I turned the Cub toward our compass heading. The first problem occurred. The compass would not hold still for me to read it. The delicate float swung, jiggled and bounced, and the fine markings went by the lubber line, first in one direction then in the other. Tom made one comment and lapsed into silence. He noted that in order for the compass to be read, the airplane must be flown stably, straight and level. I continued to climb, in a general, easterly direction. I changed headings several times, chasing the compass. Each change of heading sent the compass off again. I compromised on anything between one hundred and one hundred sixty degrees. So much for precision navigation.

When we reached two thousand feet, I retrimmed the airplane into a configuration known as cruise climb. We flew at normal, cruising power, but converted some of the airspeed into additional lift to continue a slow climb. I could see Tridelphia Reservoir, about two miles ahead. I expected we would reach it at twenty-one minutes past three, but pulled up my clipboard to make sure: distance to Tridelphia, eight miles; estimated time en route, six minutes plus five minutes for the climb to altitude. Seemed okay. We were nearing twenty-eight hundred feet; a wide, puffy layer of clouds lay above us. Tom broke his silence. "What do the FAR's say about clearance below clouds?"

There were many more clouds than I expected to see, and they extended everywhere.

"Well?" asked Tom.

"Okay," I said. The nearer the Cub climbed to the clouds, the less puffy, the more cottony and webby they appeared. The bellies of the clouds were tinged with brown. Wisps of cloud fanned by us now.

"Okay, what?" asked Tom, again.

"Five hundred feet clearance below clouds," I said.

"Well?" he insisted.

"Okay," I said, and I retrimmed the airplane to go back down again.

We passed over the brown waters of Tridelphia. We were to the left of course; I estimated by a quarter of a mile. I noted the time and managed to mark it in the log. The numbers came out chicken tracks. The compass began swinging again. I became distracted by an idea that I refused to let go: that the sight of the clouds above us were not done justice by the neat symbols of the weather report. I had taken in the idea without considering what the idea really meant. Never mind that the clouds were lower than four thousand feet, bunched and not scattered. When I saw them up close, they were real.

The phrase, "five miles in smoke and haze," brought home its particular immanence too, right then. Five miles meant you can't see. It meant the horizon was indistinct and disappeared in miasma. It meant the sunlight was filtered, diffuse, and refracted; the air had glare to it, presence, light from everywhere, in a bronze or copper cold relief. It was as the world appears when you see it underwater: distance simply disappearsed, and features seemed to loom before they reached configuration.

By Route 29, we had gone fifteen miles and already I was off my course. We had passed Howard Duckett Reservoir, damming the Patuxent River; passed it on time. We crossed Route 29, on time. The point of the problem was: where had we crossed it. I had used, for checkpoints, all the north-south arteries between Washington and Baltimore. I knew them all from having driven them. I conceived the course as a land lubber would. The references ran north-south; our course line ran from west to east. Had we crossed the highway north or south, or even on, the course? I tried to estimate the distance to the reservoir. It lay below, behind the right wing. It should have been two miles, or was it four? I pulled out the chart. What did two miles look like from twenty-one hundred feet?

I had underestimated the difficulties because I conceived of them in sequence; in fact they seemed to happen all at once. I had to keep flying the airplane. I had to watch the gauges. While I was looking at the reservoir, we lost a hundred feet. The engine was racing; the tachometer was too high; the compass would not sit for me. The more I wandered in the sky, chasing needles, altimeter, compass, airspeed, tachometer, the more the needles went to wandering on their own. Trim. Add power. Reduce power. Retract trim. More back-pressure. Less back-pressure. One minute I held a heading and the compass settled down, then a bump of air nudged the plane and I overwrought the controls to set us right again, while the compass went a waltzing. "Pick a point on the horizon," said Tom. "Pick two points, near and far, and line them up."

I pulled out the chart again and held it up, to read details, only to see the edges and pleats of the chart flutter in the wind. The wind crept into the cockpit, and the air swirled and swirled up dust. For every second I looked at the chart, to find a place, or find it again in the vibratory blur, I missed that second away from the controls, away from the horizon, from the airspace. The airplane wandered when turned free.

We crossed Interstate 95. Where, in its thirty mile length from Washington to Baltimore, had we crossed it? Route 1 lay below us now. Where was Laurel? I could see the Baltimore Washington Parkway, ahead, below the nose of the plane. It, too, spread in a line from right to left, a perfect checkpoint had we been flying north or heading south. I saw a cloverleaf spinning off the Parkway. I looked on the chart to find the cloverleaf, some clue. The details I did not expect to see become the ones most difficult to find. I looked up at the compass. The numbers and lines on the compass card were swinging by the lubber line again; east, east: northeast, eighty, seventy-five. This was beautiful. I pulled the Cub around to the right. Look at the world. The world was real. I was seeing it as if I were born today.

Real trees below us; how strange they looked. This was my familiar terrain, Prince George's County, Maryland. How could it be strange? Real roads, real cars, so tiny. Real houses, subdivisions, construction sites where the earth lay gouged and brickish, the soil red with iron. I could not find the cloverleaf. I could not find any checkpoints. I was lost. My desk wasn't moving when I memorized the course. No wind had swirled the chart then, no vibrations, no drumming; there was nothing to control but my balance in a steady chair.

I looked at my watch. What did the numbers mean to me now? I pulled up the clipboard. Nothing made sense. Where should we have been at this time? What time? I had forgotten already. I looked at the compass. One hundred forty degrees; swinging again. I levelled the wings. Where was Fort Meade? I looked through the haze. Because I knew its name I thought I could recognize it. But its name was not stamped on the earth. If I saw Fort Meade, would I know it? Tom had long since ceased speaking to me.

Out of the left window, I found my place. Very suddenly an apparition materialized. I saw first the threshold, then the numbers, then the span of runway 04, then the airport boundary and terrain. Baltimore! The thought seized on me, clutched me up. We were flying across the threshold of runway 04, at Baltimore Washington International Airport. The haze unveiled it. The runway receded into the distance. It looked like a cannon, the airport like a monstrous, grey battleship. Runway 04 was the reciprocal of runway 22. Runway 22 was upwind, active; we were in the path of departing aircraft. The line of Boeings, the never-ending string. Controllers in the tower could see us on their scopes, some God-forsaken blip.

The back of Tom's head was matted with sweat. He would not look at it. He looked out the window to the right. He wanted to see the one that comes out of the sun and clips us from the blind side.

I could not make the Cub go any faster. It was like a dream. Putt, putt, putt, putt. United, Eastern, Delta, American, National. Putt, putt, putt, putt. Thank you, gentlemen. I turned the Cub to a heading due south,

It all went away. It was a bad dream. The haze swallowed the bad dream, the vision receded, returned to gloom. Some words of Bill Paille echoed in my thoughts. "When they come out of there," he said, meaning the pilots of the airliners during take-off, "They're so busy working their computers and reading the newspaper, they'd go right through a Piper Cub. "What was that?" one would say. "Aw, just some old tin cans or something."

I was holding a heading of one hundred seventy degrees and held it for several minutes before I realized how easy it was now to hold a constant heading. Things changed after Baltimore. Now the ship was welded to my will, and both of us were vulnerable. I picked up the chart. I wanted to find the Severn River. We had been north of the course by nearly five miles. The wind on our heading attacked us almost directly from the right. The eastward drift was visible as the airplane headed south.

I saw an inlet ahead of us. From the flat perspective, its ragged coast appeared to match the chart's depiction of the Severn, inland. Tom still had not spoken, for quite some time. I held the heading. I rechecked the chart. Doubts of everything I saw pervaded me.

Not all moments of fate are so cruel. All at once, the sun broke out, shone clearly, and visibility doubled. Off the right side of the nose, south of us five miles, the sun's light shone on the roofs of the buildings of Annapolis. The city appeared gold, attractive beyond description. The waters of the Severn appeared beside the city, gleaming. The sky was radiant with light. I turned the Cub more southerly still, and left the inlet to the north of the Severn behind.

We resected our originally intended course when we crossed the Severn. I picked up Route 50, leading east from Annapolis, and followed it toward Bay Bridge. The bridge stood out ahead of us. Far below, a mile of traffic backed up. It was a usual Friday afternoon. People went to the Eastern Shore. How quickly things changed in the air. One hideous aspect dissolved, and the environment resumed in new light. The bridge appeared, luminous and fair. The weather had turned fair, the sky clear. And I could smell the sea.

The Cub is such a beautiful airplane. How easily I could perceive that it fit, that it belonged there, as part of that scene. Gulls flew around the airplane, as if we were a gull. The bay was beautiful and blue. Sailboats pecked the skein of waters, marked it with wakes. Sails were full.

On the far shore, by the foot of the bridge, I could make out the airport, Bay Bridge. The entire terrain of the Eastern Shore was different. I felt as if we had crossed a country, not a county line. The land was sandy, the shrubs were evergreen. We passed over the top of the airport at two thousand feet. Tom became sociable and stirred in his seat, as if to admit that we had made it after all. The runway of the airport lay east-west, and there was no question that the wind came from the west. I circled the airport and came back again. I had discovered a problem of a different sort. The wind T indicated that the east-bound runway was active. "What are you going to do?" Tom asked.

I circled the airplane around again. Social law conflicted with common sense. "I'll land downwind," I said.

"What would you do if you were landing downwind and you saw another airplane landing the opposite way, upwind?" he asked.

"I'd put the power on and fly around," I said.

"And what would you do if you came in to land upwind and you saw another airplane landing downwind?"

"I'd do the same thing," I answered him.

"Okay," he said. "Now, what are you going to do?"

"Land upwind," I said. And he was satisfied.

After we were down and had taxied back to the service area, my whimsy emerged. I felt we had survived. We should do something to celebrate while we were here. Tom let me go and buy a Coke.

A twenty year old woman attended to the plane. She had never seen a Piper Cub before, and didn't know where the gas tank was. Tom filled the tank himself. I paid the woman. "Where bouts in Connecticut are we?" I asked.

The woman looked at me, a little bit confused. She looked at Tom. She looked back at me. "Oh, for Lord's sakes," said Tom, "Don't pay any attention to him." She walked away.

I thought it was very funny. Tom didn't think so. Tom sat on the wheel of the Cub and folded his arms across his chest. When I finished my laughing jag, he told me to chart a new course for the trip back. He wanted a two-legged course that would take us first to Beltsville, then to home. "I'm not going to lose my instructor's license on account of you," he said.

I got down on my hands and my knees, on the pavement of that modest new airport, and I spread out my chart, I took out my pencils and my plotter, scratch sheets and computer, and I made out an entirely new log. The sun broiled me. It radiated off the asphalt and showed no mercy. Perspiration plipped from my forehead and splatted on the chart. Each time I looked up at Tom, the glare was so fierce l could scarcely make him out. He was sitting, implacable as Buddha, arms folded over his chest, on the wheel of the Cub. "Be patient," I said.

"I'm patient," said Tom.

At last, I had my new course done. "Do you want to check it over?" I said.

"Do I want to check it over?" asked Tom. "You're the one who's going to use it. Do you want to check it over?"

"I think it's right," I said.

"Then let's go," Tom said.

The return trip was almost directly into the sun. Visibility forward deteriorated. I relied on my figures for estimated time over the checkpoints, and I did a steady job holding heading. A tremendous rush of excitement lifted me when we arrived over Beltsville, exactly as predicted, on the heading, on the time. I changed course for Davis. Tom was pleased with the way I handled the airplane now. We shared the satisfaction of finishing the flight when Davis appeared in the distance, slightly to the right of the nose of the plane. I recognized that all I had to do was hold a constant heading and our course would take us right into the pattern.

After the landing, Tom paid me a compliment. "You did a pretty good job on the trip back," he said. Since this constituted as high a compliment as Tom paid, it put me in league with Balboa, Magellan, and Cortez. I felt I had participated in a process of discovery as ancient as adventure itself.

Bill Paille began suggesting that I buy an airplane soon.

MONDAY, MAY 26TH.

Today was Memorial Day, so we had no ground school. I had been elated since Friday. Perhaps Bill was right.

TUESDAY, MAY 27TH.

Today, we were taking our second cross country. The weather was perfect. A new weather system had passed and skies were clear, the winds northwest and light. Tom told me if I did as well today as I had done coming back from Bay Bridge, he would let me fly the third trip solo. Today we were to go on a three-legged trip to two airports, both in Pennsylvania. Our first destination was Gettysburg-Charnita, a small airport thirty-seven miles to the north, northwest of Davis. It lay near the Gettysburg battlefield and was named not only for the battle but for the charnel house that kept the dead. From Charnita, we would fly to York, another twenty-seven miles to the northeast. And from York, the last leg, forty-nine miles to the south, southwest and home. I looked forward to the trip. I memorized the course. The way I felt was that today we were going interstate, today to Pennsylvania. Tomorrow the Atlantic. Move over, Lindbergh.

We took off at ten thirty. As we climbed out of the pattern, I sought to establish my heading, three hundred forty-three degrees on the compass. Only when the compass began swinging again did I remember what that experience was: to fly the plane and navigate, both at once. And I found it odd - that I had forgotten how it felt though only four days had passed. The compass swung again. I followed three hundred thirty degrees. I followed three hundred forty. I chased the numbers, and followed three twenty-five and three thirty. We were climbing, in the direction of Damascus. Finally, I relegated the heading to secondary importance. As before, Tom was silent. I began fooling with the navigation log, marking the time we took off, checking the time we should arrive at Mount Airy, the next check point beyond Damascus. It would take us ten minutes to cover nine miles.

Damascus passed. It was nearby, below the left wing. So long as it was to the left of us, I felt satisfied. According to the course, it should have been two miles to the left instead of underneath the wing. Nevertheless, I felt good; I put away the chart. Tom became restless but said nothing. I levelled off and trimmed the Cub at twenty-two hundred feet. The heading was off again, at three hundred thirty degrees. We had been following three thirty for a good many minutes. Nevermind.

I took out the chart again at forty-three minutes past ten. We should have been crossing Route 40, with Mount Airy just off to the right. I could see Mount Airy. It was several miles away. But so long as it was to the right of us, I felt satisfied. We were four minutes late crossing the highway. I deduced the delay stemmed from my winding back and forth in pursuit of a heading. Okay. Out to the left I could see the drag strip and radio tower near New Market. Those were familiar landmarks. So long as things were familiar, I felt fine.

Beyond Route 40, we entered new terrain. I saw a large lake to the left of us, and pulled out the chart to identify it. It was the reservoir east of Frederick. I put away the chart again. My next checkpoint would be Libertytown, a town of two crossed roads, seventeen miles into the trip. There was nothing to do but hold heading and altitude, hold airspeed and fly. There was nothing to do but wait, until my wristwatch told me it was time to look down and see Libertytown. Nothing to do, then, but to pull out the chart and confirm what I saw. On the numbers. On the money. Then, there would be nothing to do but to put the chart away and wait until the next checkpoint. Of course, I would have to do a little reckoning *en route*. Not everything could be considered in advance. I would have to add those four lost minutes to the arrival time at Libertytown.

Tom seemed to be enjoying himself now. I noted that at times small towns were impossible to make out from the air. Some of them, considered too small to be placed on the chart, seemed to appear larger than some others, which were prominently named. Forget Libertytown. It never materialized. It did not concern me particularly. It wasn't a primary checkpoint; simply a passing point of reference on the way to the major checkpoint, the Keymar Crossroads. At Keymar, which would pass to the right of us, a primary highway with a railroad track alongside of it would run northeast-southwest. In the center of town, that highway and railroad would intersect with another highway, which would have another railroad track alongside it. That second highway and railroad would run northwest-southeast. We would cross first one, then the other, southwest of town and then northwest. I decided to settle down and hold my original heading, three forty-three. For some reason, now it seemed easier to hold that heading, after so much trouble earlier. I concluded things were well.

We passed a cement plant, off to the right. Well, truly, I have never seen a cement plant, but I saw a gravel pit when I was a child. This looked like that. The chart said cement plant. Okay. I could put the chart away again. Even though, for whatever reasons, Libertytown did not materialize, the presence of that cement plant confirmed we were right on course.

Now, we passed over the road and railroad southwest of Keymar, though somewhat sooner than expected. That struck me as somewhat odd because we were running late on our course when we passed Route 40. It might well have been that the road and railroad we had passed were not related to the road and railroad that ran through Keymar. We would just have to wait to see if another road and railroad on the same bearings came up in the next three minutes.

Ahead, quite a way, I could see the roofs of buildings, manifestly a town, one of some size, nestled at the base of substantial green hills. It lay dead ahead. Tom looked around at me, just as I was taking out my chart. "Time to read the chart," I said. He nodded and turned to the front again.

The town ahead of us might well have been Emmitsburg.

Emmitsburg lay directly on our course, nine miles beyond the checkpoint at the Keymar cement plant. Yet we had not passed over the second highway and its accompanying railroad track. Meanwhile, there was a highway and a railroad track below us to the right, on a course converging with our own. Perhaps we did pass the second highway and railroad and I had not noticed. So we had covered nine miles to Emmitsburg in three minutes. One hundred eighty miles an hour. It may be that what I saw was the second road and railroad, and, somehow, I had missed the first. Yet I had seen the cement plant, exactly where it should have been.

Frankly - we were losing altitude - frankly, I could not match up - had to retrim, too much chart reading - match up what it was I looked at on the ground with what it was I looked for on the chart. Or was that backwards? What I was looking for <u>was</u> on the ground.

"Know where we are?" Tom asked.

We were passing over that lovely town, with mountains dead ahead of us. I rolled the Cub to the right, turning to conform to the line of the ridge. "No, I don't," I said to Tom. He nodded his head and turned his back on me again.

There was a road below us. There was a railroad. There were mountains. The town had just passed behind us. Sweat began running down my face. This was really miserable. I kept edging the airplane to the right, because the ridge line kept crowding me from the left. How could I read the chart and take my eyes off those mountains? First things first. Meanwhile, we lost more altitude. I could not just stop the airplane, pull over to the side of the road, ask directions, read in peace. I wished I were home.

Tom could take no more it. "See those railroad tracks," he said. We had flown around in a U turn, one hundred eighty degrees, and I saw the tracks at the bottom of the wing as we banked. We were heading back into town once more. I had no idea what a compass heading was. I was just following by the lay of the land. I looked at the railroad track. It went back into town. I followed it. I looked at the chart. I could make the chart do anything I wanted now. I made the railroad tracks become the railroad tracks through the town of Monterey. Any town in that area with a railroad track running through it was going to be the town below my wings. Monterey was it. Never mind that Monterey lay beyond four ridges and we had flown over no ridges today. Ignore, too, the seven miles distance beyond Thurmont to Monterey. It had to be Monterey. I saw the railroad track running into and out of the town.

I followed the railroad back to the southeast from Monterey. I would go as far as the town of Thurmont, and then turn northeast to intersect my original course over Emmitsburg. I flew a respectable distance from Monterey, half a mile perhaps, a minute of flight time. I could make time compress too, as well as distance. Now I turned to a new heading, zero three zero degrees. I did not see Thurmont ahead, but then, I'd never really been to Monterey.

The town of Emmitsburg appeared, ahead of me on the new heading. A highway ran into the town. I had just covered, in my mind, nine miles, which took but four minutes by the clock. But I no longer used the clock. I had no need of it, and made my own time. We flew over Emmitsburg at fifteen hundred feet. The crossroads lay as the chart showed, and I saw a college, prominent in one corner of town. The campus and walkways were neat, the greens bright, the buildings trim. I looked at the chart. The chart showed Saint Joseph's College, in Emmitsburg. Now, I chose to doubt everything. I doubted that was Saint Joseph's College. I doubted the town was Emmitsburg. For lack of a further recourse, I turned to the original heading, three four three degrees, and proceeded to the north, northwest of town. The roads coming in and going out were all shown. Their bearings relative to the town and to the heading of the airplane corresponded to the chart. But I was given to doubt. We passed a bluff to the left of the plane. The chart showed that.

An airport appeared dead ahead of us. If the town was Emmitsburg, then the airport was Charnita. But I had been burned too badly by my own credulity. If I landed at the airport, Tom would harangue me. What was I landing here for? Was this Charnita? I circled the airport twice, then proceeded on to the north, northwest, on the original heading. We flew over a ridge, and I saw a small settlement to

the right, a highway and a railroad track, all shown. With that, I suc-
cumbed to the evidence, the weight of doubt dismissed. I turned the
airplane back around and recrossed the ridge. I entered the pattern
for that airport, whose runway lined up on the bearings depicted by
the chart as belonging to Charnita, and whose length at twenty-seven
hundred feet matched the indication of the chart. We flew a right
hand pattern here. The bluff that spawned the ridge crowded the airport from the west. The place was deserted. The wind T was pointed
perpendicularly to the runway, directly at the mountain side.

I shot the approach and bunged the landing. The Cub hung in the
flare, then pancaked. Tom grabbed the controls away from me and
jammed in power. We came down hard and bounced.

As we taxied back, he began a beration that went on unchecked
for ten minutes. I had reached my end. Charnita was the distal point
in my career. Tom exclaimed that I was crazy if I thought I could
take off and follow any random compass heading and still maintain
a course. He explained that an error of twelve degrees in heading,
if uncorrected thirty miles, would take a plane six miles off course.
We had, today, been six miles too far south. He proceeded to the
principles of chart reading. He told me that my habit of putting the
chart away between checkpoints necessarily caused me to envision
the course as a series of episodes. He reminded me that the course
was a continuum, a line, and that it was the checkpoints that made
up the arbitrary references.

Tom continued. He stressed the need to exercise judgement when I
first realized that I was off course, at Damascus, and again at Mount
Airy. He urged me to use discretion in selecting what would make a
good checkpoint. The cement plant had been a gravel pit, and some
of the secondary roads were blocked from view by the trees. He
pointed out that angles, bends in roads, configurations of highways
and rail roads, lakes and features of terrain, were ideal as references
when seen from the air.

Finally, he suggested that if I was going to use dead reckoning I
might do well to adhere to my own estimates of *en route* time and
speed. Such estimates would help locate, not only where but when,

the airplane should arrive, and, in a pinch, they would serve as a bulwark against the fear and panicky dread that squeezed my mind today.

When he decided to skip the flight to York and, instead, return to Davis, I could have cheered. I was only too happy to get down on the runway and recompute the reciprocal of our course.

The trip home went swiftly, free of strange events. At Davis, I made a competent landing. After I tied down the Cub, I met Bill and Mina in the office. Bill inquired how things had gone. I told him I got lost.

"Tom let you get pretty tangled up, did he?" Bill asked.

I nodded.

"'Well, don't feel too bad," Mina remarked. "There isn't a pilot alive who hasn't been lost some time, and if you ever meet one who claims he's never been lost, he's a liar or he ain't no pilot."

Mina had just won a place in my heart's gratitude forever.

* * *

I found out, at dinner, that Saint Joseph's College was where Gloria's mother had gone to school. I found out, further, that it was the home of Mother Seton, soon to be canonized as this country's only saint.

WEDNESDAY. MAY 28TH.

I licked my wounds.

THURSDAY, MAY 29TH.

In class, Jim introduced us to the study of radio navigation, a method of getting around the air space that has become not only common but prevalent in general aviation. Radio navigation is a modern hybrid of ancient functions. It serves partly in place of pilotage, to the extent that you watch needles and indicators instead of features of terrain, and it has almost entirely replaced the use of dead reckoning. Of the several varieties of radio navigation, use of the Very High Frequency Omnidirectional Range, or VOR as it is abbreviated, is the current favorite. Since World War II, a network of VOR stations has evolved and now fairly covers the country. Routes between and among stations constitute the Victor Airways, which is to airplanes what the federal highways are to cars.

Some of the problems we faced at the outset in class derived from terminology. The word omni refers not only to the station, the omnirange, but to the receiver set in the airplane. You tune the omni, the receiver, but you tune in the omni, the station. The omni system works by a literal definition of a very specific device. The station radiates signals. The signals are called radials. The station radiates one signal, radial, for each degree on the azimuth of the compass, three hundred sixty in total. These radials are by definition lines that originate at the center of a circle and travel outward from the center to the circumference (there is no actual circumference to the circle; VHF transmissions are "line-of-sight," and proceed unless interrupted by the terrain until the signal dies). The omni receiver in the airplane can tune in any of these radials, assuming the airplane is within range of the station. The receiver will then indicate by a needle whether the airplane is to the left or right of the chosen radial. It will indicate by a flag - the "To From" indicator - whether the airplane is on the same side of the station as the radial selected, or whether the station lies between the airplane and the radial. In the latter case, the indicator reads "To," and in the former case the flag shows "From." By these definitions, neither the word "to" nor the word "from" has anything to do with the heading of the airplane relative to the station or the radial. They denote positions of the airplane relative to the station and the radial. Since in normal usage, "to" and "from" have to do with heading, most of us in class became confused. Jim pointed out to us, however, that if we are to know whether we are heading to or from the station we must read our headings from the compass and compare them with the radials we have tuned.

* * *

A curious effect occurred after each of my first two cross country flights. At home, in the evenings following each flight, I noticed that when I shut my eyes I saw visions of the chart and the land, super-imposed. The chart in particular was etched in a way that reminded me of the craft of wood-burning: etching figures into plaques of wood by means of fire. In both cases, the image retention remained with me two days. It provided me some indication of the intensity of sight.

FRIDAY, MAY30TH.

Today, Tom and I were going to try again for York. A build-up of cumulus clouds in mid-afternoon, however, caused each of us some doubt about the risk of being caught in a thunderstorm later on in the afternoon. Tom decided at last it was worth a try to make the flight. He had a weather eye. We could always turn back. The day was basically fair.

We took off at three thirty and established the ground rules of the flight. Tom was not going to help me. He was not even there for all I was concerned. We did not establish this rule through any formal pact; rather, simply, when I made a mention about the turbulent air, Tom pretended I did not speak, so he did not acknowledge what I said. Okay, the air was turbulent for one of us but not for the other.

During the climb to altitude I got off heading. Today, for once, I was concerned with what that meant, and corrected every time, to zero three one degrees, or thereabouts. The airplane kept yawing to the left. Rather than ride right rudder, I tried to find the cause of it and discovered my left foot had been riding left rudder. My shoe was wedged between the seat in front of me and the side panel of the cockpit, and I had not noticed the pressure although it was sufficient to account for a continuing yaw. We hustled northbound, north, northeast, on the boost of a strong tailwind, directly from the south at seventeen knots. I had not flown so fast in the Cub before. We were moving eighty-four miles an hour.

We crossed Route 40 in short order. Although I predicted the time by dead reckoning, and the prediction proved correct, it nonetheless surprised me to have moved such a distance in so little time. I made mention of that to Tom. He ignored words. The Cub was left of course.

We flew by a small town to the right of us. According to the course I should have kept, no town was there. I resisted the urge to say to Tom, "That looks like Taylorsville, doesn't it?" That eerie, prickling feeling began to tickle the back of neck. My forehead began to grow flush. I knew the symptoms, I could recall the signs. Perspiration. Closed-in feeling. Agitation. A tendency toward disruption of concentration by checking little details and performing menial chores. Reset the throttle. Adjust the trim. An inability to keep my eyes on any one place long enough to register a thought. Desire to quit.

I pulled myself out of it. I would not be that easy. The town <u>was</u> Taylorsville because the roads through town conformed to the chart, and my log told me I could not have flown beyond Taylorsville at this time. Therefore, coming up would be the town of New Windsor. Isn't that right, Tom? Tom did not say a word. He did not even look down at the same checkpoint I was looking at, for fear it might reveal a clue.

The town we approached now had a road entering from the south and two roads leaving, one to the northwest, the other one to the east. The road entering from the south crossed a railroad track. The track was shown on the chart. The chart showed the track in a peculiar bend below town. I looked down and saw that same peculiar bend. Neither of the other roads crossed the track, though one converged with it east of town and ran along the northside of the track toward Westminster. Westminster lay along my course. My course lay east of where we were. I turned the Cub to zero six zero. The wind from the south would cause us to drift northerly as we headed east, northeast. From the hazy air ahead, Westminster now appeared. So you see, Tom, with a little patience and some work…. I picked up all the checkpoints. Westminster Airport. The town proper. The major highways in and out of town. I leaned forward so that Tom couldn't shrug off the words I had intended for his ear. "I'm going to make it, Tom." He smiled. He could not deny having heard that. "Yes, indeed," I said, "We're now halfway, to York."

MONDAY, JUNE 2ND.

We took two tests in school and covered pilotage, dead reckoning, charts and the use of the air space. Computers and plotters were zapping away like crazy. The tests went on until eleven P.M.

At the end I asked Andy Chase, one of Nutwell's friends, where George has been. "George went to Alaska," Andy said, "He left in early May."

It had been a long month.

TUESDAY, JUNE 3RD.

In fair weather, with a crosswind from the north, Tom had me working on landings again today. He wanted me to master the technique for the one-wheel landing in the Cub.

I flew a dozen landings and made good all but one. On the one I missed, I carried such an exaggerated slip throughout the flare that when the Cub finally touched down and began rolling on one wheel, the wing that remained in the air, in this case the left wing, still flying, still inducing drag, pulled the ship, by its drag, around to left. The Cub veered, and as the veer tightened, the right wing nearly hit the ground. Before I could decipher what to do (reduce the right aileron, reduce the left rudder; add left aileron, add right rudder), the Cub corrected for me and settled down. The ship stayed on. I recognized I was overcompensating for the wind. My effect would have worked in a twenty knot wind. Today's had hardly scraped ten.

At the end of practice, Bill rode out to the tie-down in his cart. "You know," he said, "You did pretty good today. I think you thought there was more wind out there than was actually the case, but some from among those landings you made were as good as can be made in that ship."

I felt so good I thought my heart would burst.

The rates went up on all the planes. The Cub now rented for twelve dollars an hour, up from eleven. Bill was apologetic but explained that the cost of gasoline had risen.

Tom showed me the technique for starting the airplane when I was alone. I would be alone today. He was sending me back to Charnita. The first thing I learned was to prime the engine in the usual way, to chock the wheels if there were chocks available, and to pull the prop. through in the usual way, with the switch off. Then, instead of turning the switch on to both mags and standing in front of the prop. to pull it through and start the engine, Tom had me turn the switch to the left mag. and to stand on the right side of the airplane, with my legs straddling the landing gear strut. With my right hand I could reach the blade of the prop from behind, and with my left hand I could reach inside the cockpit through the open door.

Very little force was required. I simply pulled the blade down with one hand and the engine started up. Had the airplane surged slightly, my right leg, in front of the strut, would have blocked it. Had it really taken off and started to roll, the strut would have tripped my right leg, my weight would have shifted to my left leg, and I would have fallen into the cockpit. Bill told me an anecdote about a pilot whom he saw once start a ship like a Cub by pulling it through from the front. The airplane surged. The pilot ducked the prop, then chased after the airplane the entire length of the airport.

Bill contributed another piece of advice. He told me that since the first approach is a "cold approach," I would do well to fly one practice circuit here at home before setting out *en route*. It would, as he suggested, wake up my depth perception. Tom, too, had parting words for me. Should I get lost, he said, I could always turn south and that heading would bring me back across Route 40 into familiar terrain from anywhere I likely would be.

I took Bill's advice and flew one circuit. I kept Tom's advice in mind. I was coming to understand the maxim, that being lost was not truly being lost but "temporarily misplaced."

I took off at ten forty-two. Once past Route 40, the solitude came upon me. This was my first solo away from the pattern at Davis. I kept myself occupied by keeping myself alert. It was cold today in the Cub and I was shivering. The airplane rattled on, its noises accentuated by the emptiness inside the cockpit. It rattled on, and I talked back to it. I reminded myself of checkpoints, pilotage points, until that sense renewed itself again, that flight is fluid and performed.

THURSDAY, JUNE 5TH.

We resumed our study of radio navigation in class. Electronics are upon us. It is possible to load an airplane with black boxes and gadgets the total cost of which exceeds the worth of the plane. It is possible for a private pilot to ride herd on a dashboard full of instruments.

FRIDAY, JUNE 6TH.

I was scheduled to fly solo on my second cross country today, to Carlisle, Pennsylvania. But the winds were twenty-five miles an hour and Tom cancelled my flight.

MONDAY, JUNE 9TH.

We played a game of sorts in class, a version of pin-the-tail-on-the-donkey. It was part of our practice in VOR orientation. Jim put up a display of an omni station on the blackboard. He gave each of us in turn a small model airplane, which we were to stick on the display in the proper position and heading. To the side of the display he drew the two instruments we would have at our disposal in the cockpit, the compass and the omni receiver. On the omni receiver he drew the "To From" indicator, the "Left-Right" needle, and the Omni Bearing Selector, the device by which the pilot could select a radial from the given station. Jim would put the indications on the instruments. We would pin the airplanes on the display. For two hours the class room was a madhouse. I never saw so many confused adults.

TUESDAY, JUNE 10TH.

Gloria knew that on days when I was flying a cross country I would be calling the flight service station for a weather briefing. I had given up the habit of driving down to National. Gloria became interested in these briefings, at least in my end of the conversation, because the language was so foreign to any she had known. Gloria knows English, Spanish, Italian and French. But she would make a special effort to be in the room at times I made such calls. My end of the conversation today went: "Good morning. I'm calling with aircraft identification fourteen thirty-two Victor. Could you give me the forecast winds aloft at EMI, three thousand and six thousand, for use period fifteen hundred to seventeen hundred Zulu, please." I jotted down the briefer's reply, then continued with my next request: "Thank you. And could you also give me the Reading Terminal Forecast for the same use period, please." I wrote down that as well. That was it. I told the briefer thank you and hung up. For the next several days, Gloria would reply to all my questions with "Roger," "Zulu," and "three thousand and six thousand."

Carlisle Airport lies sixty-five miles from Davis, almost directly north. The town of Carlisle was notable to me because Jim Thorpe played football there when he was in college, and the Washington Redskins practice there in the summertime. The airport lies to the southeast of town, two miles away, while the town itself lies fifteen miles to the west of Harrisburg, Pennsylvania's state capital. During my study of the chart, I took note of two ridges I would have to cross. Those were the northern most tapering of the Catoctin Mountains. The mountains run north, northeasterly but bend somewhat more easterly, toward Harrisburg, as the range shallows out onto the eastern flats. The first ridge that my course would cross stood fourteen hundred feet, and the second, which ran parallel to the first, separated by a valley, stood sixteen hundred. Beyond the ridges, the course line would cross the town of Mount Holly Springs, where railroad tracks and highways intersected, and which lay four miles due south of the airport.

The weather forecast indicated scattered clouds at four thousand feet. I planned to fly at two thousand. Bill Paille had suggested that it is easier to follow compass headings from lower altitudes. Today's winds were light, from the south, southeast. The air was webby, with moisture and haze, but it was smooth. The clouds I saw were cumuloform.

Shortly after taking off from Davis, I encountered a problem with those clouds. They were lower than forecast, and lay diffusely broken about twenty-one hundred feet true altitude. I trimmed the airplane to cruise at sixteen hundred. Mount Airy was my first checkpoint, and I passed directly over it, on course. The compass heading of zero one zero, and the prediction of a ground speed of seventy-four miles an hour, proved accurate so far. I picked up the road between Taylorsville and Libertytown. I knew that terrain from my previous flights. I was enjoying the day. Some problems developed with carburetor ice, owing to the moisture in the air, but after several applications of carburetor heat the engine held its power.

New Windsor appeared dimly out to the right of the plane. I estimated visibility was five miles. On occasion, sunlight would break through the clouds; visibility would extend to seven or eight miles. I picked up the railroad tracks and the highway that ran from New Windsor northwest. Today, I saw the cement plant, finally, near the Keymar Crossroads, where it had always been. At Taneytown, crossed highways and railroad tracks appeared. On the north edge of town stood an old water tank, painted pale green. Across the girth of the tank, writ large in black letters, the word TANEYTOWN appeared. In earlier times, towns as a courtesy posted their names as Taneytown had done, with prominent letters visible for miles from the air, to let pilots know where they were.

Another highway and a set of tracks coursed off to the northeast, on a diverging path from mine. The whole landscape seemed summerish, and the sight recalled my boyhood. The rails caught the sunlight for a moment and reflected it. A creekbed lay hidden beneath a stand of trees. The air was warm.

Highways into Gettysburg passed by, and the landscape levelled into flats. To the left I could make out the Catoctin Range, beginning to close on my course. I picked up a checkpoint at Route 15, which ran on to the north, northeast to Harrisburg, miles beyond my view of things. The flight had gone well. I was on course and on time. I had to cross the ridges, then pick up Mount Holly Springs and fly the last leg to Carlisle. I set my mind on keeping the heading steady on the flight across the ridges. It would be twelve miles between checkpoints. The ridges began to close, ahead and to the left.

For an hour, I could have expected something I had waited on to now. The sunlight ceased to dapple through the clouds. The clouds became thicker. The farther I proceeded, approaching the first ridge, the lower the ceiling of clouds became. I had let the Cub drop to fourteen hundred feet. I felt I was being wedged from above and crowded from the left. The ridge was grey. I came back on the stick and the Cub climbed. At sixteen hundred feet the clouds were on my head. The ridge appeared still higher than I was, an illusion of refraction.

The Cub flew over the top of the first ridge and visibility from the crest of the ridge suddenly shrank. Ahead, I could barely see the contour of the second ridge, much higher. Below the plane, I saw the tops of pine trees not far beneath the wheels. I looked ahead again and I could see nothing at all but grey. No ridge, no ridge before me, no ridge behind, no trees, no valley. Nothing.

I looked to the instruments and began to count. I began to count to ten. A valley lay between the ridges. I did not want to drop down before I reached the valley. I watched the needle and the ball, to indicate a turn. I had no other reference for that. The grey swirled; no different from driving in fog. Spatially disorienting, either way. I watched the altimeter; hang steady. The airspeed indicator; immediate signs of climb, descent. Count ten. Reached ten. Counted slow enough. I pulled the power back and started down.

A thousand feet above the valley floor the Cub broke out of cloud.

The run of the ridges wedged my heading into conformity with theirs. The Cub came around, to zero three zero, then zero six zero degrees. The ridge lines lay both left and right, and the seam of the valley ran underneath the plane. I'd got myself in a jam and I was just bumping along, trying to survive. The lines of the ridges appeared and disappeared. The effects of parallax, hills sliding behind hills, contours looming from contours, defeated all scale and perspective. The compass could swing as it would; meant naught.

Then, the clouds disengaged, the ridge lines dissolved and the Cub spewed out over flattening terrain. I felt like Jonah. A small town lay ahead of me, just to the right of the nose. I turned the Cub slightly and flew over. A double lane highway led out of town. I consulted the chart but couldn't find it. A set of railroad tracks led out, too, northbound. A secondary road led out to the north along those. I looked back at the chart. It didn't quite match, but I wanted the town to be Mount Holly Springs. So Mount Holly Springs is what it was. I turned to my original heading and followed the tracks to the north.

I didn't find the airport. I found the town of Carlisle, north a proper distance from Mount Holly Springs. But I should have spotted the airport to the right of the railroad tracks before I got over the town. I looked around. The town lay just under the right wing now. An east-west freeway passed under the plane. Directly ahead lay the Pennsylvania Turnpike. That lined up in respect to the town the way the chart showed it - for Carlisle. I felt certain I had simply missed the airport, come over the town just slightly to the west while the airport lay southeast. So I turned the Cub around and began backtracking. The freeway I had passed over looped around the town to the south, so I had to follow it to find the airport. I turned the Cub southeasterly, staying above the freeway. When the town receded and lay off to the northwest, I looked around for the airport. It should have been anywhere below me or directly around, but I couldn't see it.

I believed I was compressing time again, a habit of fear. The chart showed the freeway round the belly of Carlisle, then head back north. It was a by-pass route. But the freeway below the Cub just extended on to the east. I <u>was</u> compressing time. It <u>would</u> bend north, if I didn't hurry it. I decided to relax. Better visibility would help, but things would resolve on their own. Momentarily, a second freeway came into view from the right of the plane. Its course intersected with the freeway that lay beneath the plane. I looked at the chart. The second freeway did not appear.

I split the difference in the angle the two freeways made at their juncture. One freeway diverged ahead away to the right, the other ahead away to the left. I was eastbound now. No airport. Out to the left of the plane I saw a tank farm with white petrol storage tanks. The tank farm was in the midst of an urban, industrial sprawl that developed to my view with each passing second. I saw railroad sidings, loading docks, and warehouses. A double set of railroad tracks ran beneath the airplane now. I looked back at the chart. Where - anywhere - did a double set of railroad tracks split the difference between two freeways? Right there, dummy.

The sun broke out. The sky lit up. Visibility tripled in one instant. The bronze, glistening, glinting, mighty Susquehanna lay ahead. I was at Harrisburg. The whole cityscape spread before me now. I had entered the airport traffic area, two miles from touchdown, at Capitol City Airport. They had me on their radar scopes again.

I whipped the Cub around in a U. Back out I went. Back out along the double railroad tracks. Back across the juncture of the two freeways and on across the flats to the west southwest. The freeway to the left was Route 15. "Mount Holly Springs" was Dillsburg, eight miles to the east of the real Holly Springs. "Carlisle" had been a suburb of the urban sprawl from Harrisburg.

Fifteen miles later I found Carlisle. I picked up the indications for the pattern, then shot the approach. The landing was fair.

On the roll-out, I mistook the turn-off to the hangar for the turn-off to the service area, and I rolled the Cub up to the door of the hangar, where a mechanic, working on a plane inside, looked out at me. I waved hello to him, then swung the Cub around and rolled back out again.

It had taken an hour and forty minutes to make a trip that should have lasted but an hour. The man who attended the Cub in the service area signed my log book. He wrote as an entry that I had made it. I suppose he thought I looked surprised. He loved Bill's Cub and tended it with care. He even washed the windshield. When I was set to go, he suggested a route back that would avoid the hills. He told me to fly to Dillsburg and pick up Route 15. I told him I had been there once today.

WEDNESDAY, JUNE 11TH.

Tom scheduled me for another cross country Friday, so I took the day off to rest.

THURSDAY, JUNE 12TH.

The weather became hot. We sweltered through an exam on radio navigation in class. Parklawn School turned off its central air conditioning, since school had been let out for the summer. Our room had no windows. It was nearly unbearable inside, not only sticky with heat but stale. Those of us remaining in class had become inpatient to get on with it, to the end of the course.

During the second half of the evening, Jim launched us into the chapter that covered medical factors of flight. He covered the whole chapter by the end of the night. It seemed <u>that</u> pace was fast enough.

FRIDAY, JUNE 13TH.

Today's flight would be solo to Front Royal, Virginia and back. The weather could not have been better; unlimited visibility, a few scattered clouds, winds from the west.

At the airport, Bill and Tom conspired to pay me a compliment. They were standing near the gasoline pumps while I was checking out the Cub. They were talking about me, just loudly enough that

I could hear most of what they had to say, yet not so loudly as to include me in the conversation. While I was checking ailerons and control cables, Tom was saying, _sotto voce_, "Shoot, I could enter Newcomb in that contest. He can grease on ten out of twelve." The back of my neck felt feverish with pride.

It was three forty-five before I took off, late for a cross country in a Cub. On my warm-up circuit of the field, I shot the approach and missed the flare. Kabam. I flew it into the runway and bounced it. The impact rattled the teeth of Bill Paille, who claimed he was in the bathroom but heard it nonetheless. I thought the wheels fell off the Cub. When the airplane kept rolling, however, I decided to take off again. So much for ten out of twelve.

En route, I picked up my heading, two four nine degrees. With the wind from the west, my ground speed was only forty-seven. This was my first trip to Virginia, and my first trip in a southwesterly direction. It would also be the first time over the Blue Ridge Mountains, which stood southwest.

There are two ways to read a chart when a course is southerly. You can hold the chart right-side-up, so that north is at the top and the place names are legible, in which case the course will appear upside-down and the relationships reversed. Or, you can turn the chart upside-down, in which case the angles of various features, rivers, roads, railroads, all will appear in their right perspective according to the heading of the plane, but all the place names and ledgers will be difficult to read. On the whole, I liked to see the course when the chart was upside-down.

The Cub passed over the broad flood plain of the Potomac, with the river ahead in a curving ribbon, brownish green. I felt a sense of the passage of time as well as that of place. Below me were the river towns, very old, Poolesville, Beallsville. The feeling of the land conveyed the river. From the air it was possible to see why people settled where they did, why some towns grew, and others stayed the same. I was reminded of the Ohio River, which I knew as a boy, and the Missouri and Mississippi Rivers, too. The very mood of the place seemed drowsy and perpetually summer, humid and dog-dayed in mid afternoon, mellow and deepening at dusk. I could almost picture gnats, hovering in the shafts of sunlight that sifted through the trees.

Across the river, appearances changed quickly and the land became more active, and at the same time less benign. Of course that was illusory, for it was the use men made of what they found that made me think the land itself was active, or more or less benign. The Cub flew over Leesburg, a town of the South, venerable and strong. But Leesburg has a modern beltway that rings it to the south, and around the beltway are access roads, motels, and modern condominia. What I saw was really Washington, extending to the west.

Near Leesburg, I could see Godfrey Field and several small planes working the pattern. One climbed out from the pattern and I watched it as long as I could, until it disappeared behind and below the Cub. Beyond Godfrey Field, I could see the runways at Dulles, quite distinct though Dulles was eleven miles away.

As the landscape began to rise toward the foot of the Blue Ridge Mountains, farms became rockier, pastures more inclined to banks and embankments. More of the land was given to grazing, less to cultivation. Farm ponds were prevalent, and small lakes formed above dams that blocked the many creeks. The mountains were imposing, ahead and to the right. I caught sight of the small plane again, re-emerging from below the Cub to the right. The pilot was practicing aerobatics. I watched the airplane climb against the backdrop of the mountains, then dive and pull out and climb again, until this time it broke free, white above the green skyline, and rounded over backwards to do an inside loop.

Visibility made pilotage no problem. Small towns on the slopes of the Blue Ridge appeared clearly, even at great distance. The town of Paris was my last checkpoint. I levelled the Cub at three thousand eight hundred feet, and flew across the ridge of the mountains.

To the west, the Shenandoah Valley came to view.

The temperature had dropped by fifteen degrees from what it had been when I took off. Part of this was altitude, and part was the wind. As the Cub passed over the ridge, I pulled the power back slightly and let the ship descend. The slope of the mountains fell away quite steeply, much steeper than the Cub's own rate of glide. As the ship came down, its distance from the land paradoxically increased.

I crossed the Shenandoah River at Front Royal, and could see the airport at the edge of town. I had gone from the piedmont at Davis, six hundred forty feet above sea level, to the valley floor on the other side of the mountains at Front Royal, and had returned to an elevation that was very much the same. Front Royal's airport was but seventy feet higher than the field height at home. The air became warm again. I made a sloppy landing.

At some point in the outbound course of a cross country, the tension is released. Today, the point occurred atop the ridge. Return trips seemed to zip right by in contrast. Perhaps it was because the course was a reciprocal of the way just flown. Perhaps it was the impetus of going home. Today, both factors were added to a third. The tailwind booted the Cub along at almost twice the speed.

I touched down at Davis at quarter past six. The landing was perfect. It had been, except for the practice landing, an otherwise perfect flight. I never felt so good about flying or so elated at the end of a flight as I felt, sitting in the Cub, as I taxied back toward the berth. To fly seemed worth it.

In front of the gas pumps in the service area another airplane sat, somewhat blocking my path into the berth. I slowed the Cub down and put the brakes on and stopped. Bill was there. He was talking to the pilot, a young man wearing sunglasses. The pilot had a passenger with him, an attractive young women with long dark hair. She loitered near the open door of the Cessna, the pilot's plane. The plane sat in a way that its tail was slightly in my way. I thought I could clear it to get into the berth, but thought it would be better to wait for the pilot to move it, to make sure. I waited, the engine ticking in the Cub. The conversation continued between Bill and the pilot, and showed no signs of abating. They took no notice that I was there. The young woman was not part of the conversation and she turned to watch me as I grew impatient at the wait. Too perfect a day, I think. I raised my eyebrows at the woman and nodded toward the wingtip of the Cub's right wing. Could she see it? Would it clear, if I edged ahead and into the berth? She smiled and nodded yes. I eased off the brakes and proceeded to pin the rudder of the Cessna with my wing.

That ended the conversation between the pilot and Bill. All hell broke loose. I shut the engine off. Bill harangued me until both our faces were scarlet. I hung my head. After some deliberation, the pilot of the Cessna shook hands with me and accepted my apologies. He decided there had been no damage to his airplane. A trace of yellow paint from the Cub's wing was all that showed. His controls functioned. The rudder was intact. He let it pass.

The irony of a flight gone bad at the landing chocks was one I had to endure. But "block to block" is what the book says about the span of a pilot's responsibilities on a flight.

The young woman explained she had simply nodded "hi."

The rudder on a Cessna costs three hundred fifty dollars to replace.

MONDAY, JUNE 16TH.

We took our test covering medical factors of flight. One of the interesting tidbits of information to emerge from our study was the fact that smoking impairs night vision. The weather continued to be too warm for this room. After the test, half of us lit up.

TUESDAY, JUNE 17TH.

It finally rained. Rained out.

WEDNESDAY, JUNE 18TH.

Tom took me up for what amounted to a <u>check ride</u> in the Cub. We flew through every maneuver and exercise that I had learned to date. We began with Dutch Rolls on the way toward Route 40, and on the other side of the highway we did turns-about-a-point. We did rectangular courses and stalls. On the second stall, from three thousand feet, Tom told me to put in left rudder just as the airplane was ready to cut loose. It did not enter my mind that this would cause a spin. I shoved in the rudder and the Cub stalled. The world inverted. Then, the horizon began to swipe around in front of us. Whap. Whap. Whap. Down we came, spinning like a seed pod falling from a Maple tree.

After two more spins, I told Tom that I had the idea now and we should stop. The idea I had was my breakfast coming up. Tom told me to fly us home. I think he realized what would happen next. I was directionally disoriented. We were near New Market, above Route 40, northwest of the airport. To go home, instead of turning southeast, I turned due north. A moment later, Tom suggested that I was going the wrong way, so I turned the Cub around and flew due south. Although I could see that I was over my own home terrain, I could not seem to find the checkpoints that would lead us home. It was very embarrassing, and I asked Tom to be patient. He told me he was patient. I had only to choose from among Mount Airy, Frederick, Route 40, the tank farm, the drag strip, the radio towers, the road from the drag strip, Damascus, Interstate 270, Sugar Loaf, Tridelphia. The day had perfect visibility. Finally, I tracked back down Interstate 270 and got off the freeway at the Gaithersburg junction. From there, I followed the same road I used when I drove to the airport in my car.

At the end of the morning, Tom signed my log book and I was finished with the Cub. My primary flight training was complete. I had lived in that airplane forty-nine hours and fifty-minutes of my life.

Most student pilots today stay with one airplane from the beginning of their training to the end. I liked the way Bill and Tom did things at Davis, with primary flight training in the Cubs followed by advanced training in either the Piper Colt or the Cessna 150. The rules require that a student be trained in the rudiments of instrument flight, including the use of the radio and radio navigation. The student must take his or her flight test in an airplane so equipped.

Tom gave me a choice, between the green 150 or the blue and white Colt. He made no recommendations either way, but explained some of the advantages and disadvantages of each. The Cessna was easier to fly. It was the white rice of general aviation, and the airplane favored by students. The Colt, by contrast, got out better and flew faster. The Cessna had flaps. The Colt was a little trickier to handle on landing.

The Colt struck me as proud. It looked proud. I projected my own pride into it. It was a short, barrel-chested airplane (anthropomorphically endowed), but stood well off the ground on its two long struts. I could walk beneath the wing of it without bumping my head. Both airplanes had tricycle-type landing gears - nose wheels in place of tail wheels. Both were high-wing, as was the Cub. Each airplane sat two; side-by-side. Each had a full complement of instruments. The cockpit of the Cessna was low-slung, close to the ground. The Colt had more room in the cockpit, though not much. The Colt reminded me of a bulldog; reminded me of myself, that is. After studying each plane, and the owner's manual of each plane, I chose the Colt. Tom seemed not at all displeased. He may have been wary, but I think he was glad.

THURSDAY, JUNE19TH.

In the last class of school we planned an imaginary cross country flight. Jim had us put to use all the information we had learned. We threw in everything from, pre-flight planning to engine failure in flight, from getting lost to sending a mayday distress to a flight service station in order to get a Direction Finding steer. It was a casual session. Some of us who were behind in certain assignments settled that score with Jim. Sixteen of us were left from the original twenty-one.

Near the end of the session, Jim made a comment that pilotage and dead reckoning have become a lost art, and that most pilots, should they run afoul of an electrical failure in flight and lose their radio navigation equipment, would no longer remember how to keep course or find a course by reckoning a heading on their own. It made me glad to hear this because I took some pride in doing it the way Tom taught me in the Cub, which was precisely the way Jim taught us in his class.

At the end of the evening, several of us went to the Village Pizza Parlor in Rockville. There we sat over mugs of beer and fed each other malarky until the prospect of getting up Friday morning for work sent us wobbling into the night.

FRIDAY, JUNE 20TH.

I was simply not fit to fly.

TUESDAY, JUNE 24TH.

Following completion of two phases of my training: primary flight training and ground school, with both of them ending back-to-back within a week, I fell into something of a slough, about the way I had done after I first soloed. I resisted pushing on with the next project. I resisted jumping right in again. One thing that lay ahead was the FAA written examination, to which ground school was a prelude. But the prospect of reviewing material to prepare for the written exam steepened my resistance. Jim must have known of that reaction, for he warned all of us in class the final night to waste no time in taking the FAA exam. Tom must have known, too, because he made no bones about the fact that I should come to the airport to start learning how to fly in the Colt.

People in aviation, I had come to see, are like this. Perpetuation is reward enough. The answer to the end of a long campaign is to start a new campaign. Don't stop to think, or, if you must reflect, keep moving as you do. Of course, it is the fear of letting the ardor grow dim that drives people to keep the ardor bright. And, of course, pilots understand that. If they stop to think about what they've been through, some of them won't be back for any more. And, in fact, some don't come back. But, on the whole, I think pilots prefer to keep the carrousel turning and themselves on mounts. We never run out of brass rings.

Bill kept the Colt in the hangar, unlike the Cubs which were berthed outside. Tom gave me a tour of the Colt, while Orvil, from time to time, looked on. Many of the points we inspected on the Colt were the same as those on the Cub. I felt some sense of the continuity of design from one airplane, one generation of airplanes, to another. Ailerons and hinges, hinge bolts and safety wires, cotter pins and rudder and elevators and cables, those were all features still external, open to inspection. And the same precept remained: the pin you don't see would be the one that works loose.

The Colt has wing tanks, one eighteen gallon tank in each wing. It burns 6.6 gallons per hour at cruise, about twenty-three hundred and fifty r.p.m., which gives it an effective endurance airborne of five hours. Tom had me drain the sumps beneath the tanks, and then the gascollators from the low points in the two fuel lines The Colt has a Lycoming engine of one hundred eight horsepower; an engine that Bill overhauled in order to re-sleeve the cylinders in chrome. Bill's concern for his airplanes was apparent to me by now. And for all the wear his airplanes received - something to consider in light of the fact that many of the pilots were students - they were in remarkably good shape; perfect shape, in fact, since they were dependable.

Entry to the cabin of the Colt proceeded via a step up and a door on the right side. Tom had me check the fuel gauges. Throughout the inspection, I had been dividing my attention between the tour of the airplane and notes in my notebook, for the Colt was sufficiently complicated to warrant a checklist in writing. And I knew that come the next day I flew again, Tom would expect me to do the pre-flight myself and to know the checklist before we started up the engine.

At the end of the tour, Orville made the comment that I had graduated from an airplane, the Cub, to a "flying machine," the Colt. I had heard the phrase "flying machine" before, but, until I saw the cockpit of the Colt, I thought it was a joke.

Tom had me tow the Colt out from the hangar to the grassy area beside the runway. He was encouraging me to get to know this airplane in all ways that I could. I think he sensed my trepidation. Anything that I could do, handling the airplane touching it; manually lifting the hood, draining the sumps, pushing it, towing it, whatever, all that would contribute to the sense that I was to command the ship, control it; that it was mine, me. Of course Tom was right in his suspicion, for I felt exactly the opposite of command. The Cub was friendly, the Colt, imposing, and I handled the airplane gingerly, as if I thought it might kick me or bite.

I climbed aboard and waited for Tom to come down. As I sat in the seat I began to regress and feel like a child. The longer I waited for Tom, the farther back in perceptions I withdrew. Kick and bite? It's true. The Colt was a horse. I felt as I did the first time I rode on a horse. I knew I was there for the ride. But, no, the last time I truly felt like that went back before my first ride on a horse. It went back to the first time I sat on the seat of a trike, and my legs wouldn't reach to the pedal.

Tom climbed aboard and pulled the door shut. We began an inspection of controls and instruments. It only now became apparent to me how much I had learned in the Cub, for my eyes moved by reflex to the exact locations on the panel where I expected certain gauges to belong. The altimeter and airspeed indicator were on the left, essentially as before, but I was seeing them from a different angle now, no longer having to look over the front seat or around Tom. The cluster of gyro gauges directly in front of me was almost entirely strange. There was a directional gyro, with its accompanying adjustment knob, and an attitude gyro, with its level adjustment knob. The turn-and-slip indicator was an old friend. There was also another pitotstatic instrument, cousin to the altimeter and airspeed indicator: the vertical velocity indicator. And, on the cabin post to the left, intruded an outside air temperature gauge.

In the middle of the panel sat the two radios, one on top of the other. Each radio was combined with an omni receiver. There were knobs to activate each set, and knobs to select communications channels and navigation channels. There were adjustments for volume and squelch, and dials to display frequencies. The omni sets had bearing selector rings and displays of an azimuth. Within the azimuth were left-right needles and to-from flags. The radio transmitter mic hung in a bracket on the left wall of the cabin. The speaker was overhead, implanted in the cabin's roof.

The Colt had a hand brake. There were no foot brakes. Tom warned me not to try to use my feet to stop. The brake lever extended down from underneath the panel and I would have to reach for it and pull it to stop; another new reflex to acquire, this one for my right hand. The Colt had a parking brake, which could be controlled by a knob pulled out and set after the hand brake had been applied. The magneto switches in the Colt were worked by key, much as the ignition switch of an automobile. A placard provided the airplane's identification number: Five Two Zero Six Zulu. To the side of the parking brake was the mixture control, and to the left of that, the carburetor heat control. On the right side of the panel was the grouping of gauges that monitored engine and electrical functions, the ammeter, tachometer, manifold pressure gauge, oil temperature and oil pressure gauges. There was a primer pump and two fuel gauges and a clock, which did not work. The Colt had two compasses, one a magnetic compass located on top of the panel in the middle, as it had been on the Cub, the other, a remote indicating compass, located in the wing, away from the sources of deviation. Its indications were transmitted electrically to a gauge on the panel. There were switches for lights, rheostats for dimmers. The Colt had position lights on its wingtips and tail, landing lights and taxi lights, cabin lights, panel lights, and fuselage strobes. The trim crank was overhead. The master switch was underneath my seat. I sat on the left, since I was the pilot.

We began the procedure for the startup. That, too, required a checklist to keep things straight. I adjusted my seat and fastened my seat belt. I turned on the master switch. The electrical system now functioned; the gauges came alive. I set the altimeter and checked the time. I turned off the radios and the remote indicating compass, then set the mixture adjustment to rich. I checked that the carb. heat was off, and primed the engine. I locked the primer pump and set the fuel selector valve to draw from the left tank. I pulled the brake on and set the parking brake; pushed in half an inch of throttle and yelled, "Clear!" out the window, to announce the prop. was about to turn. I turned the mag. switch over, from "off;" passed "left mag.," "right mag.," "both mags.," to "start." The starter motor growled.

The prop turned. The engine started. The noise was louder than that of the Cub. I checked the oil pressure; the needle came up. A whine filled the cabin. I asked Tom what it was. He pointed to the gyros.

We did the run up in place, at eighteen hundred r.p.m. The torque of the engine became so great that the nose of the airplane dipped, compressing the shock absorber. It startled me. Tom said relax.

We were set to go. I worked the flight controls, closed the cabin windows, set the trim. As the Colt began to roll slowly ahead across the grass, Tom reminded me that the airplane steered as the Cub did, by the use of the rudder pedals. I nodded. He told me I would probably forget and use the wheel as I would the steering wheel in a car, simply because it was a wheel, not a stick. I told him, no, I wouldn't forget. When we reached the point even with the end of the runway, and I wanted to turn the airplane to the right to get over to the runway, I forgot and turned the wheel. The ailerons deflected but the airplane continued straight ahead. "I told you," said Tom.

The take-off was a different act altogether in the Colt. Unlike the Cub, or any tail dragger, which taxies at a high Angle of Attack, and, given enough rolling speed, will fly right off the runway, the Colt, or any tricycle-geared airplane, must be rotated nose high by back pressure on the wheel, in order to achieve the needed lift to fly. The sensation to me was that the airplane reared back, something like a horse, and went in a whoosh. We made the climb-out holding seventy-two miles an hour, faster than the Cub in level cruise.

Throughout the morning, we flew over the local area. We practiced turns and straight and level flight. I felt reluctant to control the ship, to take charge of it. I felt somewhat at the mercy of its power, almost twice that of the Cub, and certainly at the mercy of its speed. From point to point over the local terrain, we covered spans of distance with unnerving quickness. My world had shrunk. Over a hundred miles an hour in cruise was over sixty per cent faster than the Cub. The airplane imparted a sense of charge to me, rather than I to it. It flew <u>hard-charging</u>. The wheel was heftier than the stick, the response heavier. The Cub responded as a leaf, light. The Colt had smack, weighed twice as much, sliced. I never realized that I felt invulnerable in the Cub, until I flew the Colt. The Cub seemed correctable at all resorts. Even a bad landing was no more than embarrassment, a blow to pride. The Colt did not surrender that. The Colt did not convey the sense that it would forgive me if I missed. I felt I was mortal when I sat in the cockpit of the Colt.

Tom tried to reassure me, but the feeling emanated from nerve endings, neural circuits and viscera; no amount of reassurance copes with that. I saw how much finesse, how much touch, I had begun to acquire in my right hand, using the stick in the Cub, but I saw it when I saw today how little touch I had, using my left hand on the wheel of the Colt. I gripped the wheel too tightly, overcontrolled. I fiddled with the throttle and the trim, couldn't settle down, chased needles. My eyes couldn't find familiar haunts on the panel; the gauges seemed out of place. Tom took over, lest I blame it on the ship. He gave a quarter crank to the trim, levelled the wings, readjusted the engine speed by ear, then sat back and took his hands and his feet off the controls. As the Cub would have done, the Colt did, too. It flew straight and level on its own.

WEDNESDAY, JUNE 25TH.

Today, we practiced stalls, precision turns, and turns-abouta-point. It was a good workout, covering an hour and forty-five minutes. Since the air was fairly smooth, and the winds were light, I picked up the turns-about-a-point with little difficulty. It was experience enough simply to fly turns at an angle of bank of forty-five degrees. The sensation of banking, particularly in the turns to the right, seemed more pronounced in the Colt. The fact that Tom and I sat side-by-side now, and he to my right, contributed to the sensation, for the airplane's center of gravity lay between us, and in a tight, right-hand turn I was in fact being thrust up into the air, as on a teeter-totter. As we came around in the turns, Tom would lean back in his seat so I could see by him and out the right window, as much looking down as looking out.

I was impressed by the amount of back-pressure I had to hold in order to maintain an altitude during turns. The actual deflection of the elevators may have been no different in this ship than it would have been for the same turn in a Cub, but the strength needed to pull the wheel, to get the nose up and keep it up throughout the turn was appreciably greater. Tom recommended that I get used to using trim more often in the Colt. My left shoulder ached. I had almost forgotten that flight was physical.

The stall characteristics of the Colt differed, too, from the those of the Cub. We didn't break cleanly into a stall in this ship. The Colt simply rode up, quit flying, and lazily returned to a nose-down attitude. It reminded me of the phrase, "easy as falling off a log." It was an easy ship to work with, innately stable.

During turns-to-headings, Tom encouraged me to begin using the attitude gyro for reference. The instrument not only displayed a model of the airplane with reference to the horizon, but also indicated angles of bank and degrees of nose-up, nose down pitch. If the little model airplane in the instrument rode above the horizon line, then it meant the Colt, too, was riding with its nose high, above the horizon. If the little model banked to the left or right, it indicated that the Colt, too, was banking to the left or right, by corresponding degrees. The attitude gyro, or artificial horizon as it is also termed, was the principal instrument for instrument flight, for it pictures a similacrum of reality that, under instrument conditions, a pilot could not see.

Tom had me fly seven hundred twenty-degree power turns at sixty degrees bank. This was the steepest bank I had flown. Tom wanted me to get the feel of the Colt operating near its limits. Centrifugal force doubled our weight, the plane's, Tom's, mine. Heavy in the seat describes how it felt; even my cheek muscles sagged. I flew with the trim cranked in and full power, yet the airplane barely held eighty miles an hour and I was still hard back on the wheel. The Colt was dragging at its weight; the wings at a very high Angle of Attack. The turns could have gone sour easily. They felt wicked. The little airplane on the attitude gyro was hard over, and well above the horizon line. We had to cage the directional gyro, to keep it from tumbling in its case.

Tom loved that kind of air work. I felt relieved to be done with it; it drained my strength.

At Davis, we began work on landings. From the very first approach, I was in trouble. Tom helped me through the first time. We were using runway 08. On downwind, at a point even with the end of the runway, I came back on the power to fifteen hundred r.p.m. I cranked in trim and held eighty. We made the turn to base and then the turn to final, still holding eighty. On final, I pulled the power off, and, as the glide slope steepened, I came back on the wheel to bring the airspeed down to seventy. The airplane began wambling. Stall speed was fifty-four. I cranked in one more round of trim. We were to hold seventy until the flare. Differences from the way the Cub behaved became apparent. The Colt did not glide as well as the Cub. In fact, as Tom would say, it sank like a rock. That sink rate changed my perception of what the runway looked like coming up, and that, in turn, changed my perception of when to start the flare. The steeper slope required a greater change in trajectory, from the glide through the levelling out into the flare, and, on my first approach, I missed the entry and bounced the airplane off the runway. On the roll-out, I dug in my heels for the brakes. But, of course, they weren't there and by the time I found the hand lever and applied it, we had used up all the runway and run off through the grass. Tom shook his head. I could see his thoughts as clearly as if they were printed on his forehead; mirrors of my own. It was going to be a long summer.

On subsequent approaches, I recognized the Colt had less response at seventy than the Cub did at fifty; that it loafed like the Cub but would not correct like the Cub. I recognized that I was so nervous I was clenching the wheel. Yet, paradoxically, the wheel required a lighter touch than did the stick. And that was nowhere more apparent than in aileron response; the wheel turned as easily as power steering in a car. The aileron response was quicker in the Colt. The elevator response required more strength. I recognized I was sitting higher off the ground in the Colt. The wheels kept making contact sooner than I expected. When I perceived that, after running the airplane into the ground several times in row, I began attempts to correct by coming back hard on the wheel. I reached the stage where I was pulling the wheel all the way out to the stop, nearly as far as my breastbone, to get the ship to float and flare. But the response was less dramatic. The ship was nose heavy and I couldn't produce a quick, nose high rotation. Tom pointed out that I would never get the nose up in the Colt the way I had in the Cub. The center of gravity in a tricycle-geared airplane was forward of the main landing gears. In the Cub, or any tail wheel airplane, the center of gravity was behind the main gears.

After five times in a row of flying the ship into the runway, I started coming back earlier on the wheel. The absolute, precise, right second was required. I came back too early and too-hard now, over-correcting to the opposite extreme. The ship flared in time but with so much time overrotated. It ballooned back up and hung.

"It's a matter of timing," I said to Tom.

"It sure as hell is," he said back.

FRIDAY, JUNE 27TH.

It rained. I have begun flying approaches in my head again.

TUESDAY. JULY 1ST.

Tom wanted to know when I was going to take the FAA written exam. I told him I would take it when I finished my review.

Today we worked on radio navigation, take-offs and landings. A front had swept through and cleaned up the sky. Visibility arched into the distance as far as the eye could perceive objects. A curious magnification occurs when air is so clear. Distant objects seem much closer than they seem normally. The tank farm by Route 40, eight miles away from Davis, seemed from the air about two. Damascus, which was five miles away, seemed an arm's reach, a short glide. The steeple of the church in Damascus, still my favorite of all check-points, seemed bright as an icicle. I could see all the way, beyond Damascus, to Frederick. I could see Tridelphia Reservoir, nine miles away, as if it were a puddle by a sidewalk. I could see the tower of the National Cathedral in Washington, thirty miles. I could see the line of the Blue Ridge Mountains to the south of Harper's Ferry, forty miles at least, and trees, not only contours, but colors, greens, and shapes of individual trees as well, on Sugar Loaf, where those trees stood out against the sky.

It seemed ironic that on a day like that we practiced radio navigation.

We tracked to Frederick, the site of the nearest station. Tom showed me how to fly a course reversal when we passed over the station. We flew a ninety degree turn to the right at a standard rate of turn, three degrees per second, then a two hundred seventy degree turn back to the left, again at standard rate. The maneuver brought us back over the station the second time. It put me in mind of the game of polo. The horse is fast, the ball elusive. Maneuvering an airplane around in hundred-mile-an-hour turns in an attempt to stay over a point on the ground you cannot see except for its depiction, by needle and flag, on an instrument's display forced my awareness, for the hundredth time, that flight is live. The needles bounce, jiggle. The wind is live, quick, and upsets the plane. The airplane is mischievous; it will run away. While you look at one thing, something else takes off on you. Airspeed drops. Altimeter shows climb. Too much back-pressure. Upset in the bank - five degrees, six degrees - and you're warping the radius of turn. The compass is swinging. The omni needle is swinging. Compute ninety degrees to the right of the three hundred twenty-degree radial; compute two hundred seventy degrees to the left of fifty. The ball showed us skidding outside the turn. "Too much rudder," said Tom. The altimeter showed we were losing altitude now. Retrim. The heading came around. You never stop. You don't arrive and stand there, okay, I made it, like a runner on first base.

We broke off from practice and shot four landings at Frederick. At Tom's behest, I flew the approaches at seventy-five instead of seventy, and landed the plane each time with some degree of accuracy. Tom concluded that the extra five miles an hour in the approach speed made the ship firmer to control in the way I had grown used to in the Cub. It gave the ship responsiveness to help me check my errors.

We took up tracking the omni again and tracked from Frederick to Davis. With the wind behind us, we flew at a ground speed of one hundred twenty miles an hour and reached Damascus in under five minutes. We reached it so fast, in fact, that when I saw it, below the left wing on this day of perfect visibility, when I saw the school and the shopping center, and the church with its steeple, and the road that ran out of town to the south, toward Laytonsville and home, I said to Tom, "That's not Damascus, is it?"

"I don't know," said Tom, "You tell me."

WEDNESDAY, JULY 2ND.

Tom confided to me that he did not know why I could not land the airplane.

We had a lovely day today, less Tuesday's brilliance.

I knew why I could not land the airplane. I was afraid of the landing. I flinched.

We agreed that I should practice landings until I learned. Omni tracking, instruments and other skills would have to wait. From the top of the first approach, when I trimmed the ship to glide, I felt the jitters in me arise. But this time I removed myself from my own concerns and watched my own responses. Jittery. I watched how abruptly my right hand snaked up and grabbed the trim wheel, how roughly I cranked it around. I watched how my vision darted from place to place without settling long enough to derive a sense of track or slope. I watched how my tight grip on the wheel produced a jerky turn to base, and how my left foot plunged in on the rudder and produced a skid. I noted how unsettled my responses were when we came down the slope on final, how I yanked the throttle closed, how I paid no heed to the horizon, to the levelling of the wings, how inattentive I was to the sense of the airspeed. I observed that the tension in my left wrist rolled the wrist slightly to the outside, a matter of a degree or two, and how that wrist roll translated through the wheel to an aileron roll, and the ship rolled left. No sense of power, no sense of the engine, no sense of the airspeed, no sense of the attitude, no response to the track or slope. My eyes had not found the point of touchdown on the runway. My eyes should have locked on that point by now, determined the points beyond it that rose in the windshield in perspective, the points ahead that dropped away in perspective, that showed we would clear the fence, the threshold, the first hundred feet of the runway and then flare. The Colt required that touch. The less well I flew it, the tighter I became. And, in the flare, I blinked.

On the second time around, I relaxed. If I could not learn when tense, I could as well just bounce them on at ease. So, I flew one leisurely. I made believe the cockpit was equipped with pieces of fragile glass, and I could damage any one of them if I handled it too roughly; I pinched the wheel now between my index finger and thumb, about the way I hold a teacup. I adjusted the throttle and treated it as the fine tuning instrument it is, very gently. When I wanted more trim, I turned the wheel politely, instead of cranking it around. And rather than read instruments and let my gaze just jump from place to place, I looked at the way the world around me looked, and watched the runway coming up. The ship greased on. Tom scratched his head.

We flew landings for two hours and tried them in all sorts. I made some power-off, starting the glide from the downwind leg, and some power-on, to stretch out the approach and shallow out the slope right up to the flare. We worked on slips, steep approaches, fast approaches at eighty, bleeding off airspeed; approaches holding seventy-five, approaches holding seventy; seventy in a glide, seventy with power; sixty-five with power. "You're a strange one," said Tom. "You do one thing wrong and then another, then everything clicks and you've got it." He signed my log book and got out. I went on to fly four more by myself.

FRIDAY, FOURTH OF JULY.

TUESDAY, JULY 8TH.

Boning for the written test.

WEDNESDAY, JULY 9TH.

I took the written test today. Heat and putrid air, those hallmarks of a Washington July, were on us for the sixth straight day. The exam center was the FAA regional office at National Airport. In the windowless room where I took the exam, an air conditioner recirculated the smog. There were sixty questions, all multiple choice. Many of the questions involved computations, and many of the questions were sequential, with the answer from one question providing the premise for the next. The test took me two hours and forty-five minutes to complete, and by the time I left the building my eyes were bloodshot, the effects of strain and polluted air. Outside, I sat on the bank of a hill and watched the jet planes burning kerosine.

FRIDAY, JULY 11TH.

Rained out. It cleaned the air. Tom called and wanted to know how I did on my test. I told him I did fine.

TUESDAY, JULY 15TH.

I have become preoccupied again with shooting landings in my imagination. I have not flown in thirteen days.

The weather today was fair, the winds, northwest and bumpy. Tom asked if I had received my test score yet. I told him no. It would take ten days.

We flew dual, and practiced take-offs and landings. It marked the first time I had flown the Colt in any wind. We had fifteen knots at forty-five degrees crosswind from the right, on runway 26. After an hour and twenty minutes of watching me bounce them on, Tom concluded I was rough, but safe and got out to let me fly alone. I flew six more, no better.

WEDNESDAY, JULY 16TH.

Tom was going on his vacation at the end of this week. He and his young woman friend, Paula, were flying in his Taylorcraft to an airshow in Oshkosh, Wisconsin. This relieved me of the compulsion to finish by July. Tom would be gone two weeks. When he came back, Gloria and I would be leaving on our vacation, the first two weeks of August. I took the day off.

FRIDAY, JULY 18TH.

This was Tom's last day. He wanted to know if my test score came back. I told him no.

I had a talk with Bill before I started flying today. I asked him, in my own fudging way, if, someday, after I had my license, he would let me fly the Colt on week-end trips; cross country as far as New Hampshire, where we had friends, or Cincinnati, where I had family.

Bill replied, in an equally fudging way. He said I ought to buy a plane myself.

We had a cross wind directly from the north, ninety degrees from the right on runway 26. The wind matched Tuesday's in strength and gustiness, fifteen knots. It put a chill right through my guts. Tuesday's wind was quartering; today's was the ninety degree cross wind I had feared to land in. "Think you can handle this wind?" asked Tom. By that, he meant he would like to have sent me solo from the start.

"I guess so," was my best, equivocal response. I tipped him off. I had too much pride to say an outright no. "Okay," Tom said, "I'll ride around with you a couple of times."

Either he heard the sigh escape my lips, or else he had heard the pounding of my heart.

We took off in the Colt. The cross wind required one-wheel

landings. We had to establish a slip to the right into the wind, and hold the slip, hold opposite rudder and the right wing low, from final on through the flare out, through the point of touchdown, and on into the taxi roll. I had done it in the Cub but never in the Colt. The turbulence made it all the harder to control the ship, and all the harder to control the slip. I smacked a few on. The Colt wallowed and wambled in the gusts and downdrafts. On more than one landing I failed to hang in against the crosswind, reducing the slip too much in the flare so that the ship began to sidle to the left at the point of touchdown. The tires let out yelps each time, like wounded pups.

When Tom got out, I lapsed into my habit of letting the airspeed climb on final. I started bringing the ship into the flare at eighty. I excused the habit on grounds that the indicator needle of the airspeed indicator bounced in the turbulence, which of course it did, and would not settle down, which of course was also true. But, in fact, I liked the speed, for at eighty the Colt was solid to control. If I was too late coming back on the wheel in the flare, at eighty I would not cut through and fly it into the runway. There was speed to pay off into lift. Several times I ballooned back up; I was starting to land long. The flares themselves were long, the space required to use up speed. The wind today saw the limit of my skill.

* * *

In the mailbox at home I found my test result. It had in fact arrived today; I had spoken too soon to Tom. The envelope came from Oklahoma City. Inside the envelope was a computer card. And on the card I saw a perfect score.

TUESDAY, JULY 22ND.

Nerves. My nerves were completely on edge today, gritty with anxiety about the wind. I was so adept at judging the strength, direction, and quality of the wind that I needed only look out the window from my dining room table and watch the leaves on the Walnut tree outside the apartment and I could tell exactly what the approach slope would be at Davis. Another cold front had gone through last night, and winds today repeated Friday's. There would be another ninety degree cross wind, at fifteen knots with turbulence, on runway 26.

I arrived at the airport and checked out the Colt. I began to perceive now what the lump of anxiety was really all about. It was Tom's presence, or his absence I should say. Whether he flew with me or not, when he was there in the airport his presence reassured me. I knew that he knew what I was doing, even if I didn't. Tom gave me that support. Today, though, I was on my own. He was a thousand miles away today. For me, today would be a preview of the day when I would be a private pilot, showing up at an airport to take out a plane.

On the other hand, I found some strength in the routine of an established procedure, and I relied on that routine today during the pre-flight of the Colt. I went through my paces with self-conscious care. Even the words I spoke to Mina and Orville had ritual benefit for me. By the time I was into the airplane, I felt reasonably secure.

Such confidence translated immediately into mania. I started flying approaches right off the bat at eighty. Within a few approaches I was up to eighty-five. The Colt was, literally, tearing in, eating up runway. I was becoming wilder, responding to the wind with a mood in kind. Yet, I became intent on the point of touchdown as well, greasing them on, as the only criterion for the landing. The touchdowns were soft. The approaches were savage, but I finagled the airplane to a soft touchdown each time; perhaps technically a grease-on no matter the disqualifying, jittery, jumpy, herky-jerky flare out from final that sometimes floated on and on for as long as three seconds, while I payed off the airspeed. Touch down soft and keep running hard. All the way to the end of the runway, grinding at the brake to bring the ship to a stop.

Again, I sometimes failed to check the drift and landed, soft but with wheels sidling, not headed true to the direction of travel. Tires barked. The Colt was suffering me. I came in once high, hard, fast and failed to pull the throttle all the way back to the throttle-stop. I didn't know I hadn't pulled it to the stop. I thought I had. I did not see the tachometer, which showed the prop. still turning at a thousand r.p.m. I dumped the Colt over into a slip that devoured over half the runway. Why wouldn't the ship sink? Why would it not come down? I finally got it down - could have flown a missed approach - decided I could make it down and entered in the flare. The airplane floated for a hundred yards before it touched, softly, mind you, and then kept running hard before the nose wheel touched down too. Without the nose wheel on the ground, no brakes. Without the brakes, express train toward the fence. No room to take off now. The nose came down. I hit the brakes. The ship ran out of runway. I stopped before I hit the fence. And only then, stopped, did my ear tell me what my addled brain refused allowance for: the engine was turning too fast, dummy. You left the throttle part way in.

As I taxied back, I hardly knew what to say to myself.

Bill came out of the hangar on his golf cart. It reminded me of a starting pitcher about to be yanked. The relief pitcher was on his way in from the bull pen. The manager was coming now with the hook. I waited at the hold-short line. The cart arrived and went underneath the wing, then reappeared by the door. I put the parking brake on and opened the door. Bill had a smile on his face. It took restraint for him to smile at this. "Slow down," he yelled, "You're way too fast."

I nodded yes. Bill turned the cart around and drove away. I closed the door and let off the brake. The next time down, I slowed to seventy-five.

At the end of the practice, I felt very good, extremely good; because I had survived. I told Bill in the office that the air was so bumpy that on one approach I flew up out of my seat, tugging at the seat belt, and hit my head on the roof of the cabin. He did not seem impressed. Instead, he talked to me at some length, very courteously, about the advantages of landing the Colt slow. "You can bring that ship in at sixty, holding power until you're sure you're down, and cream it on," he said.

WEDNESDAY, JULY 23RD.

A mix up over scheduling.

FRIDAY, JULY 25TH.

It rained.

TUESDAY, JULY 29TH.

Today was hot, from the very break of dawn. The air was fine with the haze of heat. Not a movement of air stirred among trees or shrubs as I climbed into my car to start the drive. By quarter past nine, I was in Laytonsville, turning onto the road toward the airport. The haze and heat and stillness of the day presided over the countryside. I had been over this route, through this town, so many times now. This part of the drive, the last two miles from Laytonsville to the airport, this too worked ritually on me. To fly was to perform live, on stage, before no audience. My anxiety each time at the thought of performance bled out into the countryside. It was as if by seeing signs in place I could allay a fear, prepare for something else. My eyes moved reflexively from point to point along the route. From the Exxon station in town to the sign by the road that advertised fresh eggs. I had come to know the trees that overhung the road, had watched their progress into foliage from the early spring. I had come to know which pickup trucks I'd see, coming the other way from Damascus, en route to Olney, Gaithersburg or Rockville. I had come to place Leek's barn, and the woods behind that. I considered it a good omen to pick up a hitchhiker, on days that one appeared, in dungarees and clodhoppers, heading toward Damascus. Good omen; a good deed returning same. I spotted the cows in the shade of the trees, and judged the farmers by their crops. Get-it-together-time for me. I turned the radio off. I put away my cigarettes. Sometimes, I said my prayers, while waiting out the moment for the airport to appear.

Today the ritual went bad, reversed its normal course, and woke the opposite effect I had expected it to have. It sprang loose thoughts. I thought: it isn't fun for me. I really don't enjoy it. I don't like to fly. I thought, further: it would be very simple. I could just simply arrive at the airport, get out of my car, I could go into the office and greet whoever was there, and say, excuse me, a moment, please, a word. I want to quit.

That thought took no more than fifteen seconds to be born. It came out whole. From the roadside sign for the farm fresh eggs, to the prospect of Leek's barn, the thought had fully formed. I felt surprised that such a thought could form so fast, with so much force; subjunctive and conditional, as could, I could do it, to conditional problematic, now as would, would I, will?

By the time I reached Hawkins Creamery Road and saw the airport on the left, and turned, I had the problem on my hands. With the ritual near its end I faced the consequence of choice. In fifty seconds time I would be face to face, with Orville, or Bill, or Mina, one of three, down early to open up the shop, to open up the office just for me. I watched myself resolve.

The Paille's car sat in the parking lot. It was Bill or Mina. I went inside the office. It was Mina here today.

I said hello and Mina said hello, and I expected her to stand still and wait for me. I expected her to comment on the day, the weather, the heat, to say a word of small talk, to invite my further response.

But Mina would not hold still to comment on the weather or the day. She had another day in store for her. She opened the door from the office to the hangar. She turned on the hangar's lights. She moved one place and then another. Did a chore and then another. This silent side of aviation here; the shirttails of her green plaid sport shirt out; her eyeglasses loose on the bridge of her nose. She turned the compressor on, to work the hangar door. She turned the switch that raised the door. The hangar door rose, like the curtain. Day invaded the hangar now. The Colt stood, nose to the door, as if it were waiting, animate, to go out.

Clearly, Mina. would not stop for me. Today's the day, like

yesterday, deep in the heat of another summer month. There were the chores. She slid the wheel chocks away beneath the Colt. She fetched a towing bar from the wall, from among the hangar's tools. I'd wait. I'd stand and watch her do my work for me.

Excuse me, Mina. I took away the tow bar from her hand. I hooked it to the Colt's nose wheel myself, and pulled the airplane out myself. There was no stopping Mina, here today. And, had I waited any longer, she could have towed the ship right to the line.

IV.

Before leaving for vacation, I had achieved my twentieth hour solo. It took two and a half months of flying to get there. Three-quarters of that solo time went into take-offs and landings, which was making time the hardest way of all. Two-thirds of the time was spent in the Cub, and that included the cross countries. At an estimate of one landing every six to ten minutes of solo time, I had compiled a hundred solo landings now. Not odd at all that nearly each one was etched in my mind. I could compare the experience on grounds of intensity to that of writing; performances were almost equally brief, developments almost equally slow.

By my return to the airport in the middle of August, with the hump of summer crossed, I was happy to see Tom again, and he, I think, was happy to see me. We were renewed in our enthusiasm.

TUESDAY, AUGUST 19TH.

Tom and I flew dual, on a day both humid and overcast. He introduced me to a maneuver called "flight at critically slow airspeeds." That meant, we flew all morning at seventy miles an hour, a speed not far above the stall. We worked around New Market most of the time and I kept picturing in my mind the image of a dog dogpaddling. It fit the Colt. We were flying nose high and though, of course, we had no paws, we were scrambling nonetheless to stay afloat. Tom would have me climb at seventy, then hold an altitude at seventy, then turn to a heading at seventy. Then, he started putting the maneuvers together:

climb and turn to heading at seventy, level out, then descend and turn
to another heading, still at seventy.

I had begun watching the instruments today, for Tom was using
the practice to lay the a foundation for instrument flight in days
to come. I had to take care, not to over-bank, so I watched the
attitude gyro in the turns. To coordinate headings with climbs and
descents, I watched the altimeter and directional gyro, both. The
directional gyro gave a sense of the rate of turn, as did the degree of
bank given by the attitude gyro. The rate of turn provided cues for
timing, when to start the roll-out from the turn. The idea of coordination applied throughout the instruments. I watched airspeed,
altimeter and tachometer to regulate the engine speed. I used trim,
and learned to make finer adjustments on the throttle, to regulate
descents, climbs, and constant altitudes. I learned to be responsive
to finer changes in the back-pressure, for it was the wheel, the elevator control, that held the airspeed constant in this work. By the
end of an hour, I was able to arrive at an altitude, on a heading,
both at once.

We broke away from slow flight, and Tom introduced a new
ground reference maneuver: S-turns across a road. We used Route
40 for the road and worked eastbound from Mount Airy toward
Baltimore. The road was under construction along several segments,
and there were yellow barrels placed at regular intervals beside the
sites. They provided ideal references for the maneuver. Tom brought
the Colt down to seven hundred feet above the ground, fourteen hundred on the altimeter, and stepped the power up to cruise. We crossed
the highway perpendicularly, northbound. Once the highway lay out
below the wings on either side, Tom banked to the right and began
to make the turn. By correcting for the northeast wind, he made the
turn at a constant radius. A yellow barrel formed the center of the
turn. Tom framed it in the struts of the right wing, as he would have
in flying a turn-about-a-point. As we came across the roadway again,
this time southbound, he levelled the wings and rolled smoothly into
a bank to the left. We repeated the maneuver, this time picking up

another barrel, until, at the end of the full S, we had crossed the road again, heading north. The crews looked up at us.

Tom had me try it. I underbanked the upwind turn, immediately lost my sense of the wind, slued back in an overcorrection and came across the road diagonally. The crews went back to work. As I went into the turn to the left, I drifted too far out, and, then, intent on the barrel, I banked too much until the left wing blocked my view. By the time I had straightened, the Colt had climbed two hundred feet.

When we finished our air work, I flew the pattern for runway 08 at Davis. Tom had me pull the power off, from a point on the downwind leg even with the end of the runway, essentially as we would have done in the Cub. Since the Colt sank straightway, our approaches were necessarily short and somewhat steep. Tom wanted me to get used to that, landing dead stick. He told me to make a point of landing that way from now on. The purpose was for me to learn to evaluate the slope.

WEDNESDAY, AUGUST 20TH.

The weather continued humid and overcast. I flew solo all morning in a review of Tuesday's air work. It marked the first time I had taken the Colt outside the pattern by myself. I felt at ease and flew the ship well. I was beginning to feel in the Colt that sense I had acquired near the end of my hours in the Cub, that when I flew the ship solo I was really not alone. The airplane kept me company.

FRIDAY, AUGUST 22ND.

It rained. I showed up at the airport anyway. Tom sent me home.

TUESDAY, AUGUST 26TH.

The weather turned fair again, the air swept clean by northwest winds.

When we were ready to go, Tom sent me into the office to get the hood. It made me laugh. I knew it was coming. The hood was a device worn for instrument training. It was a plastic visor, completely opaque, with a long, open snout. The purpose of the hood was to cut off the view of the outside world, and it did just that. When you put it on, you could not see outside the cockpit of the airplane. All you could see were the instruments and controls.

We took off and, during the climb-out, Tom took over the ship while I fitted on the hood. We were still climbing to altitude and turning toward our heading, northwest, when I said good-bye to Mother Earth and entered the world of the instrument board.

I took over the controls again. The attitude gyro became home base to me now. It interested me, these segments and removes of reality. My body was moving at seventy miles an hour, incorporating the motion of the plane. Yet I was still in my seat, myself not in motion at all. Oh, except for movements, the slightest gestures of the hands and feet; my left hand on the wheel, my right hand on the throttle; almost imperceptibly those move. But my eyes did move, my gaze shifted. It shifted actively in this small world, as if it stood for the act of flight that the gauges represented. As if the world, from instrument to instrument, was moving all about me. The little airplane in the attitude gyro goes up above the horizon bar. We're nose high. The airspeed drops to sixty-five. Nose high and slow. The altimeter is approaching eighteen hundred feet. Nose high, too slow, and in a climb. I let off a little pressure on the wheel. Now, the directional gyro begins its slow procedure, the numbers and heading markers slipping by the lubber line, ever so innocently: three hundred thirty-five degrees, and now three thirty-three; then three-thirty, and on to three twenty-eight.

"Hold three forty," said Tom, whose voice intruded on my private inner world.

The little airplane lay banked somewhat to left. It meant we would be turning slowly left. My gaze moved from gauge to gauge, like a bee among flowers.

"Three forty," said Tom.

I felt cut off, removed from that. It was a very pleasant feeling, whose sole quickness was expressed by the muscles of the eyes.

"Move your eyes faster," said Tom. "Scan." How did he know how fast my eyes were moving? He could not have seen me, nor I him. I was hidden inside my hood. "Don't linger on the gauges," he said. "Scan. Hold three forty. Level off at twenty-one hundred feet. Hold seventy miles an hour."

Suddenly, my world had turned into chaos. The attitude gyro depicted the little airplane, no longer high above the horizon bar but, rather, on the bar, and, then, below it. Below the bar and in a bank, forty degrees to the left. And here I thought we were upright. I thought we held a steady climb. I should have listened to my ears; they heard the engine revving up, the wind begin to shrill around the struts. I rolled the wheel to the right and pulled it back. The little ship came up and perched upright again, above the bar. The airspeed dropped, the engine's revving subsided.

When everything was right, and we were stable, I checked the heading. It seemed to me we still were heading north. I had not felt a turn. The numbers on the gyro might have winked, so subtly had they traipsed on by. The heading was one eighty now. I'd turned the Colt around due south.

We continued instrument work until I established two routes, both soon to be reflexive for the eyes. The gaze would travel from the attitude gyro to the airspeed indicator to the altimeter before returning back to the root of the chord, tonic, as it were, the attitude gyro again. From there, the second route proceeded, from the attitude gyro to the directional gyro and back to the attitude gyro again. Intermittently, the other instruments were taken in a sweep, the tachometer, manifold pressure, oil pressure, oil temperature. Eventually, Tom would have me expand the routes to include a whole new segment, the omni, which I'd learn to track on instruments.

Tom gave me two tips that helped. He suggested that I look at a gauge with only a glance, and then move on before I thought about what I saw. My mind would carry a visual retention of what the gauge had shown. The image would persist long enough for me to interpret it while my eyes were moving *en route* to the next gauge. The second tip he gave related the attitude gyro to the directional gyro. So long as the airplane flew wings level, it would not turn. Since the directional gyro depicted turns from heading, I need not consult it so often, provided I had a constant idea of the ship's attitude. If I saw that we were level by the attitude gyro, I could assume the heading would not change.

I began to tire. We had done climb turns and descending turns and level turns to headings. We had done slow flight, at seventy, itself tiring to me because the controls became so soft. The world of abstract information, instruments, had begun to teem, like a filmed documentary of ants in an anthill. The charm of close focus gave way. I began chasing needles. I began to feel on the verge of being overwhelmed. The inside of the hood developed glare, which seared my eyes. Perspiration covered my forehead. I could have been at work with a pick and a hoe. Abstract information was, at its worst, a tidbit of information here, a unit there. Here, move the left foot in. There, now move the right. Okay, move the eyes to the left and down. Carry that bit of information to the hand. Pull the left hand. Contract the muscles. Extend the right hand against that knob, three-eighths of an ounce pressure, no more. Stop.

"Take off the hood," said Tom.

I took it off. Lord, but the world outside was bright! I had been gone only for an hour.

WEDNESDAY, AUGUST 27TH.

The weather continued to be fair. The winds had swung around from the southwest, and the air had become unstable.

Tom put me under the hood from the moment we took off. I did the climb-out on instruments and headed northwest from the pattern. Today, I brought my chart. It lay on my lap, folded open to a square that encompassed our local area. The chart was not to give me reference to terrain, since I could not see the terrain. I brought it for a reference to the omniranges, at Frederick and Westminster, because Tom was going to have me fly back home today, entirely by working on the instruments. We flew northwest for fifteen minutes, following the heading Tom gave. I held the ship at twenty-one hundred feet, cruise speed. I could estimate from past experience more or less where we were. With the winds southwest, we would be across Route 40, somewhat northeast of Frederick, perhaps around New Market. At the end of fifteen minutes, Tom told me to take him home.

The first thing I did was scratch my head. No matter how prepared I made myself, the prospect seemed bizarre. One thing at a time; a matter of sorting things out. I went back through the regimen. I had to establish where we were. To do that, I had to tune in Frederick, and then Westminster, take bearings, and see where those bearings crossed. While I tuned the omni, I had to fly the ship. Four hands would help but two would have to do. Smooth air would help, but today's air was bumpy and unstable. The needles of the gauges jiggled in the chop. The wind upset the Colt from even keel; I fought the wheel. Three or four times in ten seconds I would spot for attitude off the attitude gyro. Fifteen or twenty times a minute, every minute of the flight; nine hundred to twelve hundred times an hour, the muscles of the eye coordinate to spot one gauge. If the Colt banked right, expect a change in heading to the right. One to two times every ten seconds, the directional gyro is taken in a glance. Every heading change required correction, a second glance for rate of turn, a third to time the rollout, a fourth and fifth to settle down again. Every change in attitude, with nose below the line, meant airspeed on the rise, altimeter decline. I caught the airspeed in a glance, maybe fifteen times a minute; nine hundred times an hour. The altimeter the same. The turn and slip indicator, as needed, was often when I flew. And, now, the omni figured in. One more set of knobs to tune. One more gauge to scan.

I tuned Frederick, finding its frequency from the chart. I thought I had numbers in my mind, 109.0, but in the pace of flying blind the memory had erased. I could only think in attention spans of thirds and quarters and fifths of seconds now. Most bits of information here were obsolete in seconds. The abstract ciphers changed too fast. Four seconds was a span of time. A minute was a week. Nothing was automatic, except the assurance that the airplane would get away from me in three seconds if I took my eyes away from it for four. I held the chart in my right hand, held it up to the snout of the hood, so I could see. Reading a chart for its printed matter was difficult in flight. Vibrations made it blur. Reading it while under the hood was worse. And the air today was full of chop. While I was trying to get Frederick's frequency, while I was trying to find Frederick, period, the Colt hit a bump and I flew up against the restraining belt, and hit my head on the roof.

I glanced forward at the gauges. The gauges had come alive in a burst of animation. It was the story of the toy maker and his factory full of toys. When the toymaker was gone, the toys begin to dance and play. They were playing now. The little airplane was jigging, topsy turvy. The airspeed needle was off on its own, up to a hundred and ten again. This was what is known as "steady as she goes." Altimeter, now unwound a hundred feet. The heading markers swung by on the face of the directional gyro, swung by and *dos-si-doh*, and swing your partner the other way again.

I leveled out. I retrimmed. I applied back-pressure and gained back altitude. I turned the ship, recouped the heading, counted the numbers like lost sheep. I have a second free? Good. I snaked my hand to the radio and turned on the omni. The amplifier hummed. Static and garble issued from the speaker. I turned the volume knob down. I turned the squelch on. I heard the wind again, beginning to rush; the prop. was turning faster, the engine speed was up. What were my little friends doing? Back to the gauges. What's going on here? Scold them. Plead with them. Please, hold still.

I tuned the channel selector knob. One zero nine zero popped up in the display, digit by digit. Frederick issued from the air. But was it Frederick? I had to identify the station code. I flicked the identifier switch. Morse code began to sound out the letters FDK. The code repeated and repeated, dot dot dash dot/dash dot dot/dash dot dash. I picked the chart up again, located the station for the second time, looked inside the printed box and saw the station code revealed: FDK. That was it. I turned the code switch off. The Colt hit turbulence and jolted me. I looked at the attitude gyro. The little airplane was banked hard left; the heading was gone again.

First things first, and that was first. Next, to get us home again, select the radial from the station that crosses where the Colt was at that moment. I tune the omni bearing selector. The flag showed "to," then showed "on the line," then "from." The needle swung and centered: Zero seven zero degrees from Frederick. Where on that line of position were we now? Repeat that procedure with the omni at Westminster.

I picked up the chart to find the station frequency for Westminster, 117.9.

The little airplane had dipped below the bar again. When I found Westminster, tuned it in, identified its code, and took cross bearings for a fix, I would find out where we are, or were a moment ago. By then, we would have have left Frederick's radial behind; the information obsolete.

The tachometer was down to twenty-two twenty r.p.m. Consult the altimeter, it was twenty-one eighty. Airspeed was down to eighty-nine. We were in a climb.

From there, we would just turn around and head to the nearest line of position and track from either station to Davis; from Westminster on the two one five radial, or from Frederick on the one four zero radial.

Right now, we were heading north, turning west, and in a climb.

From there it would be easy.

A gust abruptly rocked the Colt. The airplane entered in a dive. We turned back east.

Easy. Track the omnirange to Davis, shoot cross bearings on the way.

The tachometer was up, to twenty-four hundred again. The airspeed had just passed a hundred twenty-eight.

Cross bearings for the point where both radials intersected, above the airport, naturally.

"Hey, Dave," yelled Tom.

"Yeh?"

"How you makin' out in there?"

"Okay."

FRIDAY, AUGUST 29TH.

Tom put me under the hood again for the third day. We did air work, reviewing turns, course keeping, and turns to heading during climbs and descents. To my surprise and pleasant satisfaction, I found I did not tire so quickly. My eyes had learned their routes. Holding the plane on instruments had become reflexive.

Tom put me through some stalls. We did them in all varieties, power off, power on at fifteen hundred r.p.m., power on at cruise, straight ahead, and out of turns to left and right. The stall on instruments was weird without a view of earth. The little airplane appeared to ride up, higher and higher above the bar in the attitude gyro (the appearance is false; strictly speaking it is the bar that drops lower and lower in the gauge. The little airplane is fixed, though the eye never records it that way). The Colt teetered precipitously, the teetering sensible by feel. The engine labored and there was no mistaking the amount of back-pressure on the wheel. Then, the ship cut loose, the pressure on the elevators decreased, and we went over the top. The little airplane in the gauge seemed to come down as if deflated until it dropped below the bar. I relaxed back-pressure on the wheel. The airspeed quickly picked up from fifty to a hundred. I put back-pressure on the wheel again and watched the little plane rise to the bar.

Tom was pleased by the way I flew the Colt today. He announced that we would now try unusual attitudes, a euphemism for inanity on instruments. The point of that was to teach me to recover the ship should I be on instruments and, for any reason, lose control. I was to look down at my lap while Tom flew the plane. He would put it through maneuvers of all sorts, then tell me to look up at the instruments and take over. It seemed to me that I had achieved a number of unusual attitudes on my own the day before, without Tom's help at all.

I looked down at my lap. I put my hands palms down on my thighs and waited. Tom took over the controls. He began gyring the Colt through some turns. I tried to follow by the sense of balance, acceleration, inertia of the inner ear. It was not possible to do. Every time Tom cros-controlled the airplane, the contrary motions lied to me. I became spatially disoriented; what was up? what was down? It seemed we moved backwards for a while. I was sensitive to Tom at work on the controls. He worked his hands and feet quite hard. The power settings of the Colt altered several times; engine up, engine down. The maneuvers grew more violent. The airplane heeled over, apparently to the right; then yawed, it seemed to left. It seemed he put us in a dive. No, then it was a climb. I was slammed around in my seat. Centrifugal force tugged at my jaw. Then I was slammed against Tom, then back against the cabin wall. Suddenly we stopped, in mid air, I was quite sure, and I felt my stomach rise. "Okay," said Tom, "The airplane is yours."

By reflex, my feet shot to the rudder, my hands to the wheel and throttle, my gaze to the attitude gyro. The little plane was well below the bar, hard over to left. I gave the Colt right aileron and came back on the wheel. The airspeed dropped from a hundred ten to cruise. The little airplane, its wings levelling, rose to the bar again.

"That's good," said Tom, just so pleased. We went through another sequence. This time, he gave the ship back to me on the verge of a stall. I caught the little airplane well above the horizon bar, just at the instant we cut loose. I relaxed back-pressure and ran the power up. The ship came down, the speed returned. We levelled out again. Tom could not say enough about how pleased he was with me. "We'll try a hard one now," he said.

I gave him the controls and sat. I daydreamed while he ran us through the works. We banked, we slammed around, we turned, slipped, skidded, turned the other way. It was not possible to follow this. His legs pumped the rudders. His elbow flailed while he worked the wheel. "It's yours," he said.

Like a gunfighter's draw, I went for the controls. But where was the horizon's line now? Gone! Gone from the gauge! How long could I wait, before deciding what to do? I judged it was a stall. I jammed the throttle in and ran the wheel forward. "Nooooo!" Ear-splitting cry came through the cabin, through the hood. Tom wrenched the wheel away from me and pulled the throttle out. He came back hard, hard on the wheel. The G force mounted, I felt my jaw and cheek flesh sag. The airspeed crested at a hundred thirty-five, then gradually began to fall. The horizon line appeared again, from the top of the gauge. No stall. I had shoved us over into a vertical dive.

TUESDAY, SEPTEMBER 2ND.

Was the day after Labor Day.

WEDNESDAY, SEPTEMBER 3RD.

I knew what the windsock would look like long before I saw it. That bright orange tube was erect on the pole. Northwest winds at fifteen knots. Tom sent me out to solo in the Colt.

FRIDAY, SEPTEMBER 5TH.

Orville said to me that when you land at night at Davis the runway looks like a postage stamp. Orville used to land on decks of carriers when he flew for the Navy, so Orville ought to know. Tom said that the first time he landed at night at Davis he was so unsettled by the sight of how small and inaccessible the runway appeared that he considered going on to Montgomery County Air Park and landing there. I said to myself, however, several times during the week, that if the runway at Davis was two thousand feet long during the day, then it would still be two thousand feet long at night. Tonight, we were to start on nighttime landings.

The day was lovely, the evening, too. I showed up at the airport at seven-thirty. Mina was at work in the office, Bill was sitting outside the hangar with two friends. Several planes were active in the area. I checked out the Colt in the hangar. Tom was gone, flying in his Taylorcraft. When I finished with the Colt, I joined Bill and his friends and used a soda pop case for a chair. There was a haze in the air, so typical of the waning summer dusk. The winds were from the south and balmy. One by one, the planes came home. As the dusk began to deepen and to fade, I spotted Tom. He greased it on.

Something gentled us as we sat and talked. Something in the air affected conversation. Speech was tranquil, everyone humane. Mina put the runway lights on. I expected the lights to have been bright, brilliant even. They were not. They shone no more brightly than the lights on Christmas trees. Tom tied down his airplane and walked across the airport toward us. The friends of Bill rose to say goodnight. Bill commented that he was glad to see the summer at its end. The shortening days meant shorter working hours for him. Mina appeared and wanted to know if so-and-so's airplane was down yet. None of us knew. She trekked down the taxi strip to look for herself. The outlines of the trees across the airport dimmed now. Tom arrived and decided we should wait until it became fully dark before we left. I decided not to smoke, recalling what I had learned in ground school about cigarettes and night vision. We kept our backs to the open hangar, avoiding the few sources of light within it, since night vision was delicate, easily impaired. On the far side of the airport, the ships in their tie-downs glowed faintly, like markers of graves. Mina returned. So-and-so was down and had already gone home. It takes half an hour to accommodate darkness and see. Tom said he'd close the airport up after we were done. Bill and Mina bid us goodnight.

When we were ready to go, Tom sent me to his car to get a flashlight. Should the Colt's electrical system fail, we would be without lights in the cabin. Without lights, we could not see the airspeed or the altitude, the compass or the gyros.

Before we started up the engine, Tom prepped me on procedures for our landings in the dark. We would not use the airplane's landing lights, for Tom felt they tended to draw your gaze to the focus of the beams ahead of you. Instead, he asked me to imagine a series of cords stretched across the runway. Each cord was drawn between the runway lights on either side. The cords were eighteen inches off the ground, the height of the stanchions. "When we come in for the flare," he said, "You try to split the difference between the first two runway lights, and imagine tripping the 'cord' with the wheels. When you trip the 'cord,' you start the flare. Apart from that, you hold power on the approach until you know you're down, and you hold a minimum altitude of nine hundred feet on final. No lower than that until you're sure you can reach the first set of lights on a glide. Nine hundred feet is two hundred fifty feet above the terrain, and that will give us clearance."

What Orville had said, what Tom said, too, was true. We took off and, on the climb-out upwind, I got my first view of the airport. The wind had blown us to the right of the upwind leg and Tom had told me to look back at the airport to see how we tracked. I looked back from the window. The airport lay below the left horizontal fin of the tail. The runway consisted of two small strips of lights, blue and twinkling, like distant stars; "Well?" asked Tom.

"I see we've drifted off our course," I said.

"What about the size of it?" he asked.

"It looks like a first-class postage stamp to me," I answered.

The smoothness of air belied the wind. The wind was strong, and batter-smooth in its consistency, so typical of wind at night. A small strobe flashed from the roof of the hangar; from altitude it was the only reference. Tom claimed it was not fully dark. I claimed it was. The runway lights were barely there to see. The runway itself was nothingness, the black hole between the rows.

My eyes kept searching out by habit for the cues below the plane, cues I needed now to fly the pattern. The cues were gone. The houses, the backyards, laundry lines of the subdivision, the stands of hard-wood trees, pasturelands and fences, fields plowed into furrows, none of these were visible. In place, new sets of cues, all strange to me, appeared. House lights, streetlamps, and deepnesses of dark, confused my sense of place. The wind caused us to drift. For a moment, I lost sight of the airport. Then, the airport reappeared; the twinkling strobe atop the hangar again my reference. "I'm having trouble with the track," I said.

"I know," said Tom. I had taken the crosswind leg too far, only to find I lost the distance on the downwind leg when the wind made us drift north again. I crabbed the nose over to the right. Different reliefs appeared, unusual figurations. Whole swatches of the earth lay void.

Tom took over to complete the first approach. I had enough to learn to keep the airport in my sight. He carried the downwind leg beyond the usual point for power reduction. The runway lights lay forty-five degrees behind the left wing. Then, he pulled the power down to fifteen hundred r.p.m. The glide began. He cranked in trim, holding eighty. We turned to base a good mile east of the airport, much farther than we flew these turns by day.

On final, he stepped the power up again. It slowed the rate of sink and stretched the glide. I tried to guess where we were on final; over the field behind the house that sat across the road? The stand of trees behind the field? The altimeter dropped below eleven hundred feet and continued dropping slowly. I could see the runway lights, to the right of the nose as we crabbed to the left to correct for the wind. A thousand feet and dropping slowly. The lights began to foreshorten and flatten in perspective. We maneuvered off those strings of lights, whose every change of shape, geometrically precise, revealed our course. Tom stabilized the slope, a constant sink. The lines of runway lights neither flattened nor lengthened now, but converged in equal lengths on either side to the vanishing point at their far end. Tom held the slope. We split the darkness of the rows.

Quite abruptly we were there. Eight hundred feet, seven seventy-five. The hangar strobe flashed by. The first two lights arrived. Tom turned to true our heading with our track. He pulled the power off. We tripped the imaginary cord. He started coming back. The ship whooshed ahead, consuming a vacuum. The first two lights went by. We settled down and sank. The wheels burned on, two tiny yelps. And then the nose came down. He hit the brake. We slowed. Down, safe and sound and on. The rows were equal distance to either side, and half the length of both the rows still lay ahead. "Nice job," I said.

"Thank you," said Tom. He turned the ship off the runway to the left and we passed between two lights. With the runway lights behind us, everything now was pitch dark. How did he know where the taxi turn lay? He turned again now to the left, from the taxi turnoff to the taxi strip proper. Again, how did he know?

"Hey Tom," I said.

"What?"

"How do you know where you're going right now?"

"By touch," he said, "By feel."

We were rolling ahead over pavement, at six miles an hour. "By touch?" I asked. "By feel?"

"Okay," said Tom, "All yours." He gave the ship's controls to me. I slowed it down to two.

TUESDAY, SEPTEMBER 9TH.

We planned a cross country flight for tonight, to Carlisle for the second time for me, but this time in the Colt, with Tom, and by a different route. We were to use the omni all the way.

The weather today was fair. Another change in the weather had occurred since Friday; fronts now were coming through with increasing frequency, and those from the northwest promised Fall. Tonight's air smacked of it, the very smell of pine. Visibility was perfect, unlimited. We were wearing jackets for the first time since last May.

I made one practice approach and then took off to climb *en route*. The time was eight o'clock. We would track north to Westminster, fly over the omni, and track away on a radial to Carlisle. I had written the nav. log out in large figures, the better to see in the gloom of the cockpit. I figured we should spot the airport at eight forty-eight.

During the climb to altitude, I tuned Westminster and selected our relative bearing, the zero three five degree radial, to the station. At three thousand feet, I trimmed the ship out to cruise.

The air was predictably smooth. From three thousand feet we

could easily see Baltimore, and the glow of light from Washington. "Forty miles," said Tom, "At least." There was a network of starlight above us. I had not seen the heavens so deep in several years. To hold a heading was effortless tonight. The ship went ahead in perfect trim, with nothing to do on the part of the pilot but monitor the airspace and the instruments. The altimeter remained as if glued on three thousand feet. The engine never before sounded so smooth. No wavering patches of air of differing densities occurred to bind or free the prop., to change the pitch, or rock or bump the ship. The tachometer's hand held steadfastly to its mark, twenty-three fifty r.p.m. in cruise. The airspeed indicated a hundred and one and held, with not so much as a jiggle from the needle. The compass card no longer swung, but floated in its case, on zero two five degrees. The directional gyro stood steadily on zero two five. The attitude gyro depicted the Colt, at ease abreast the horizon bar. The entire instrument board was at rest. Even the left-right needle of the omni suspended dead center, like a willow frond in calm.

Minutes passed without a word from Tom or me; each of us absorbed in his own respective flight.

At sixteen passed eight, we passed over Westminster. The town lay off the port quarter, the only bright lights in the area. I looked at the omni display. The flag changed from "to" to "over the station," and I marked the time in my log. We changed heading, and tracked outbound. I selected a new radial for the second leg north, three five seven from Westminster to Carlisle.

Here and there the lights of houses appeared, and here and there, in stretches, the lights along the country roads. More moments passed, with still no word from either Tom or me. Later on route, I tuned in Frederick and took cross bearings. "Where are we now?" asked Tom, breaking the long silence.

"Hanover," I said, and we resumed our silence again

The lights of Gettysburg appeared, ahead and to the left, and then the lights of York, beyond Hanover and the right wing. The earth, for all its immenseness, is populous in cityscapes. More distant sites, as far away as Lancaster, and conceivably Philadelphia, seemed covered in canopies. They glowed.

The ridges lay ahead of us, completely black. They seemed to be a vacuum of existing light, even darker than the space among the stars. I took cross bearings from the station at Harrisburg, confirming our position and our track.

Few houses lay below us now. I noted the time in my log. We picked up tracking from Westminster once again.

I saw another airplane. Tom saw it in the same moment, and we both watched it, silently, drawn, I think, to its beacon light. That distant neighbor was thirty miles away from us, or more, due west.

I looked at my watch. It was eight forty-eight. Carlisle was due. I looked out over the nose of the Colt. There was Carlisle, a string of blue lights perpendicular to us, dead ahead.

I pulled the power back and let down from altitude. We arrived over the airport at twenty-one hundred feet. "Which way are you going to land?" asked Tom.

I could not see the sock or T. "Land west," I said.

"Why's that?" he asked.

"Wind's northwest," I said.

We came around to the south again and let down to pattern altitude, circled back to the right and entered the pattern. I flew a long approach and let down quickly at the end of final. The Colt flared, the wheels rubbed on. "Put the power on and go," said Tom.

I pushed the throttle in. The Colt took off. "What's wrong?" I asked.

"Nothing," said Tom, "I haven't had my dinner yet."

FRIDAY, SEPTEMBER 12TH.

We were scheduled to do the last bit of night flying tonight. I needed twenty-five minutes and three more take-offs and landings to meet the requirement, three hours, ten take-offs and ten landings to a full stop. The weather was bad all day but the forecasts all called for clearing by sunset. Tom said he would phone me by six o'clock, before I left for the airport, to tell me whether to come out or not. He called at six. He said don't come. At six forty-five, by sunset, the weather cleared.

TUESDAY, SEPTEMBER 16TH.

The FAA also requires students to make at least three solo take-offs and landings at an airport with an operating control tower. I had known for a week that we were going to try it today. Tom said we would go to Martinsburg, West Virginia, forty-six miles to the west of Davis. He assured me that of all the requirements for a license, this would be the easiest. That appears to be my cue to make things difficult. For a week, I began building up a case of nerves, and over the week-end I reviewed the AIM for operating procedures at a controlled airport. Martinsburg was no great shakes, certainly it was not Dulles, National or Baltimore. But, as the hour drew near, it seemed not to matter. What bothered me emerged as the fear I would not understand the radio transmissions from the ground controller. Hence, I was afraid I would have to admit to the controller that I didn't know what was going on. I recalled that Jim had said in class that if you don't know what the controller wants of you, then tell him. Tell him that you're a student pilot, tell him that you don't understand, tell him that you're a stranger at the airport, ask him to repeat or spell things out. The point was: don't be proud.

Tom, too, had given me some help with that. He counselled me to expect a reply from the controller that would be in keeping with the request from the pilot. That narrowed down the field of directions a controller might issue to just those two or three likely possibilities. Radio use is highly tactical.

When I arrived at Davis, Tom decided that the weather was not fit for the flight across the mountains to Martinsburg. We would fly locally instead, so I could practice, under the hood.

We took off, and I went on instruments in the climb-out. The air was very turbulent, which added appreciably to the difficulties of instrument flight. We headed northwest and worked on precision maneuvers, climbing and descending turns, and unusual attitudes again.

Tom told me to take off the hood and track on the omni to Westminster. We had been burning fuel since take-off from the right-wing tank. The Colt had not been flown often in recent weeks by pilots other than myself, and since I rarely flew more than two hours at a stretch, and always used the left wing tank, Bill and Tom were concerned about condensation having gathered in the right. We had less than a full tank in the right wing when we took off. Now the gauge was about on the peg. I tuned Westminster. "Bout time for a switch to the left tank," I said to Tom.

"Not yet," he said.

I confirmed the code from the station and selected a radial to the station. The needle centered and I turned to heading to begin to track on it. The wind was northeasterly. Above our heads lay a broken layer of cumulus clouds. Through it, at times, the sun broke out and shone down on us. Out the window to the left, I saw the gravel pit I had so long ago mistaken for the cement plant, a distant part of my career. "Know where you are, I'll bet," said Tom.

"I do, indeed," came my reply.

I had my hands full with the wind today. Tom was amused to see me having to work to keep a course. We were tracking the one hundred-dred degree radial "to" the station, but the wind, quartering from the left, caused tendencies to drift. I crabbed to the left but could not find a heading that would settle us on course. We drifted to the right. The left-right needle deflected to the left. I crabbed back to the left, the needle centered, but I overflew the course, and the needle deflected to the right. I reduced the intercept angle, hoping to find the one heading that would hold us on- course, but we drifted to the right again, recrossing the line in a constant weave. "Having your troubles?" Tom inquired.

"Well, we'll get there," I said. The needle in the fuel gauge lay on the peg now. We hit a bump. The needle bounced and showed some life, then dropped back and lay on the peg again. It troubled me to be using an empty tank.

Zero nine zero was the best heading I could find. To hold the heading constant, on the numbers, was the hardest thing to do, for the wind upset the airplane, and each tilt from even keel produced a turn from heading, ever so slight, and the drift to right, or over-correction to the left, began all over again.

"You're chasing the needle," said Tom.

"No joke."

"Let me." He took the controls. I sat back. He tracked to Westminster as if the air were ideal calm. I watched, with some degree of awe, as Tom taught me how to fly the plane again. He sliced the headings one degree at a time. I counted myself skillful if I could hack off five. He used the airplane as if it were as razor blade. When the left-right needle centered, he froze it. Any bump that occurred, he swallowed it, absorbed it in a reflex of correction that was part of the bump itself. He took the turbulence in stride. A moment went by. The heading had not changed: zero eight eight degrees. The left-right needle remained dead center, still. "That's all there is to it," said Tom. "You establish an intercept angle when you're off, and you establish a correction angle when you're on. Use the former to get you on, and then the latter keeps you there."

"Incredible," I said. He gave the ship to me again. The needle instantly moved left.

We flew over the station. I looked down and saw the white cone, built on a block house in the middle of a fenced clearing on the top of a knoll in the woods. The engine quit.

I raised my eyebrows as I looked at Tom. The propeller kept windmilling, but the engine was done. Tom smiled and sat back. The wind in the struts made a very lonesome sound.

"Any time now," said Tom.

I reached to the left and moved the tank selector valve to the left tank. Within a second, the engine came to life.

Tom put me under the hood and had me track toward Frederick.

I did much better going west, so he had me break off and practice stalls.

After I was thoroughly disoriented, the effect of half a dozen stalls accompanied by turns, Tom asked that I take off the hood and resume tracking to Frederick. What greeted my eyes when I lifted off the hood was a solid floor of cumuloform clouds underneath the plane. We were at thirty-three hundred feet. I could not see the ground.

We tracked the two seventy radial, and I held a heading of two eight two, correcting for the wind. Breaks occurred in the clouds below. Gobby, white patches gave way to green and brown patches of the land. Tom was demonstrating a point about instrument flight, radio navigation in particular, for it would not have been possible, on the basis of the few holes in the clouds, to use landmarks for pilotage. Dead reckoning would be just that if done like this. While I mentioned those original observations to Tom, and he nodded, amiably, replying, "Uh-huh," and "is that right?" the omni flag changed, now showing we were over the station. Then, it changed from "over" to "from." I thought the indication was a prank. "You did that," I said to Tom, for it occurred to me we had arrived too soon (I had forgotten we had wind behind us now; our ground speed was quite high).

"Did what?" asked Tom.

"You changed the omni bearing ring."

"I did not," he said, amused, perhaps, because I thought him capable of that.

I looked at the bearing selector ring: it had not changed, two seven zero. "Then, we just flew over the top of Frederick Airport," I said.

"So?" said Tom.

"That means we're over the middle of town," I said.

"We are," said Tom.

I looked down through the holes in the clouds. Main Street winked up at me from half a mile below.

We turned one-eighty and came back over the airport. "Call in," said Tom. "Call Frederick's Unicom, and ask them what their active runway is."

I tuned the radio to one-twenty-two point eight, removed the microphone from the hook and held it in my right hand while I flew the airplane with my left. I listened, so not to jam another transmission, then pressed the transmit button while holding the microphone directly to my lips. My first official enquiry came out, "Frederick Unicom. Piper Five Two Zero Six Zulu. Say your active runway, please." I released the transmitter button and waited. My heart was in my throat, so pleased and excited was I that this would work. A woman's voice returned, very loud and harsh through the speaker in the roof of the cabin. "Piper Crigle Czurgle Sckunch. Frederick Uphflenm. Runway flrfle scgsz zact-ve."

"What did she say?" asked Tom.

"I don't know," I said.

"Tell her 'thank you.'"

I pressed the transmit button and spoke: "Thank you. Zero Six Zulu." I looked over at Tom. "What <u>did</u> she say?" I asked him.

"She said runway forty is active," he answered.

WEDNESDAY, SEPTEMBER 17TH.

Today, the weather improved to the extent that scattered clouds replaced the broken layer we had encountered yesterday, and, too, to the extent that winds were lighter, persisting from the north, northeast. We took off on route to Martinsburg at ten a.m.

I tracked on the Martinsburg omni, to relieve me of some of the navigational chores. The clouds were low again today. I had in mind the two ridges that traversed our course and that we had to cross to reach the valley to the west.

By Sugar Loaf, the cloud cover lowered to little more than two thousand feet. As we passed the north shoulder of the mountain, I let down from eighteen hundred to sixteen hundred to keep clearance below the clouds. "What'd you do that for?" asked Tom.

"To keep clearance," I said.

Tom sighed.

We approached the first ridge line ahead, the southern tapering of the Catoctin Mountains. The Potomac lay off to our left four miles. The ridge elevation reached eleven hundred feet. I consulted the chart, more than once, to check on the highest points. The clouds continued to lower.

We arrived at the ridge and flew over. Tom reached across in front of me and grabbed the radio mike. We had been monitoring the tower. Now, Tom transmitted a request: "Martinsburg tower. Piper Five Two Zero Six Zulu. Are you VFR?"

Some static squawked and a man's voice replied. "Zero Six Zulu. Martinsburg tower. We are VFR. State your position." I rushed to tell Tom our position. I looked at the chart, at the landmarks outside. I would estimate the miles.

Meanwhile, Tom had answered him: "Matinsburg tower, we're twenty miles east, flying to the omni."

While I was still looking to find out how many miles east we were, the controller from Matinsburg replid to Tom: "Advise we have a Convair and a Cherokee in the vicinity of the omni. Report from the omni."

"Zero Six Zulu," said Tom.

Now, I was about to claim I could not understand what the man was talking about; I was about to claim the transmission was garbled or the speaker in the airplane distorted his words. But I could see that I was trying too hard. Some more rational ear inside my head than the one I laid claim to, had taken note: that the receiver in the Colt was pretty good. Actually. That the voice of the controller came through loud and clear. Actually. And that what he was saying, in spite of my disclaimers of unintelligibility, inaudibility, and Mystery, was that, yes, we could get in at Martinsburg, and where were we? that we would think that we might not, and - careful - there were a couple of airplanes in the airport's traffic area. Those thoughts consoled me while we rushed the second ridge.

The second ridge was really two. They lay in parallel two miles apart, each of them a fifteen hundred footer. I let the Colt drop to fourteen hundred in the valley past the Catoctin ridge. What lay ahead were the northern tapers of the Blue Ridge. Harper's Ferry lay ahead to the left, the confluence of the Shenandoah and Potomac rivers.

The clouds were continuing to lower the farther west we pushed. I began to climb the Colt in cruise. We reached sixteen hundred feet again, and the first ridge broadened before us. The air turned webby. Individual trees poked up from the summit. The Colt skimmed over, the clouds of summer a hundred feet above our heads, the trees of early Autumn a hundred feet below our landing gear. I caught a glimpse of Harper's Ferry, serene on the rocks of two rivers' mouths, white water surrounding it below. The second ridge arrived. "Kinda' tight," I said to Tom as both of us sucked in, to help the Colt get over.

"Lord," said Tom, "Didn't it ever occur to you to fly above the clouds?"

"No," I said.

"And track the omni from up there?"

"Like we did yesterday, you mean."

"Uh huh."

"My part in that was inadvertent, Tom."

"Well, what would you do if I weren't here?"

"Turn around and go back."

The Shenandoah Valley opened out before us now. The clouds disappeared, stopped behind us where they banked up atop the ridges. Tom was on the radio again. I was looking at the sights. The countryside appeared in bronze, the effects of the northeast wind and the moisture it infused into the air.

Developments began to pour in over the radio. We were picking up transmissions from the other two aircraft in the pattern. Out ahead of the airplane, I could see the omnirange. I pointed it out to Tom. Tom was on the horn. "Roger," he said. I had no idea. what was going on.

The town of Martinsburg appeared; it seemed to be shimmering, refracted into strata. I saw the airport to the left of town. "I see the airport," I said to Tom. Tom had seen it; Tom had seen it all. The controller was on the air again. "Report to Front Royal. Contact Dulles Approach." To whom did he address these things? Greek. They were speaking Greek.

"Start your turn," said Tom.

"Runway thirty-three," said the controller.

Someone told him, "Roger," and concluded with aircraft call numbers.

We should have been using runway forty. Apparently we weren't. "Runway forty is closed," said Tom.

"How do you know?" I asked.

"He just said we're using runway thirty-three."

The airport lay dead ahead of us now; we were swinging by in a turn to the left. I saw the Convair now, glint against the sun. It was a monster, twin engine turbo-prop, banking to the right onto final. "I see the Convair," I said to Tom, then realized, on seeing Tom, that Tom had seen it, too, four steps ahead of me.

"Don't make your turn too tight," he said. We had reversed course, downwind now for a right hand approach. I was ready to initiate the turn onto base. The Convair, ahead of us in the pattern, made a touch-and-go landing and took off. "Report to the omni. Contact Dulles approach," said the controller.

I came around hard in a tight little pattern, as if I were landing at Davis. "No, no," said Tom. So, I loosened up the turn. "Martinsburg tower. Zero Six Zulu, on base," Tom said.

"Six Zulu," came the reply, "Cleared for landing, runway thirty-three. Winds light and variable. Altimeter three zero zero eight. Check gear and flaps down." We came across base and turned onto final.

"Six Zulu," said Tom, acknowledging the clearance. The Convair was long gone, climbing out into the haze. "Be alert for the wake," said Tom.

We dropped the landing on, fair. No wake disturbance encumbered the approach. While the Colt rolled out, the controller came on again. "Six Zulu, make a hard right turn at the intersection."

"Six Zulu," said Tom.

I made the turn onto the taxiway and turned the radio volume down. Our instructions were complete now, we had only to taxi ahead to the service area. As I came to think of it, everything the controller had said had made sense, while I had been too jumpy to make sense of it. We made a U-turn in the service area and shut down. Tom opened the door. I opened the window. "Well, how do you feel?" he asked.

"Nervous."

"Why?"

"Because I can't keep ahead of what's happening."

"You'll get used to it. You just have to listen in terms of what you want to hear. If you ask for clearance to taxi, the man won't tell you to report your altitude."

"Hmm," I said.

"Right?" asked Tom.

"All right," I said.

"Ready to try it then?" he asked.

"Listen, Tom," I said, in the midst of scratching my mustache. "I was reading in the AIM last night."

"Yes?"

"It says that, if you're a student pilot, you can go ahead and identify yourself as such to the controller. That controllers are instructed to be very helpful and clear when they know it's a student on the other end."

Tom thought for a moment. "Well," he said, "If you feel that way, go ahead."

"I do, Tom," I said, "My pride is dead."

And Tom got out.

The Colt sat at rest. My body sat at rest. My mind was working overtime. Time came, the sum of a long moment.

I flicked on the switches, turned off the radios, ran through the check list. The engine started. Now I turned on the radio and took the microphone in hand. One long breath, and out went my message on the air. "Martinsburg tower. Zero Six Zulu. STUDENT PILOT. Ready to taxi. Request three landings to a full stop. Over."

I released the button and waited.

There was a curious silence on the air waves.

I waited.

The seconds....

The seconds.....

Oh my God. The volume knob. I had turned it down; I never turned it up again. The thing I dreaded most, I'd done. Too late; I turned the volume up. More silence. Static. No voice. I had missed the controller's entire reply to me. I would have to go back on the air and confess.

Mercy. The controller came on the air first. "Zero Six Zulu, did you copy?"

"Negative," I said.

"Take a hard left and follow the taxi strip. Report from the hold-short line for clearance to take off."

"Zero Six Zulu," I aswered, my voice dissolving in gratitude. The man understood exactly what I did. He understood. I let off the brake and the Colt rolled out. I turned to the left. The taxi strip lay out ahead of me. The man knew exactly who I was. That made me feel much better now. I even laughed. There was a man working in the tower who was humane and wise. I suddenly felt okay myself.

FRIDAY, SEPTEMBER 19TH.

It had begun to rain. A massive tropical depression had worked its way up from the Gulf of Mexico, virtually inundating the states along its way. The warm air mass moved very slowly and seemed to park over Washington. Rains that began early in the morning came down vertically in a windless fall. By nine a.m., forty major streets were blocked by floods in the metropolitan area alone. The radio said that traffic was in chaos.

Tom wanted me to begin preparations for my long cross coun-try flight, which was obviously not to take place today. The FAA requires ten hours of solo cross country from students. Those hours could be earned in as many flights as were necessary so long as the shorter flights went fifty nautical miles away from home and the long flight covered a total distance of three hundred nautical miles. The long flight, in addition, had to be to two other airports, and there had to be a hundred miles separating each point. The final flight would be the return flight home. For a student who flies in the eastern part of the United States, there was almost too much freedom in the format of the flight. So many airports dotted the countryside, and so many changes in terrain fell within a hundred miles, that I spent nearly half a day on my hands and knees looking at Sectional Charts, which I taped together almost wall to wall across the living room floor. I computed and plotted so many cross country flights, in so many possible combinations, that, by the end, I felt tanked. I had imagined flights over mountains, along the coast, across rivers, over cities, to and from, around, Pennsylvania, New Jersey, New York, West Virginia, North Carolina, Virginia.

Too much. I settled for the trip we planned in class, the last night of class in ground school. That imaginary cross country would go from Davis Airport to Shenandoah Valley Airport, near Waynesboro, a hundred nautical miles to the west, southwest. From there, I would fly east, southeast to Williamsburg/Jamestown Airport, near the town of Williamsburg. I would have mountains, I would have rivers, I would have coasts, and history itself would unfold beneath the plane. From Williamsburg, I would fly north to Annapolis, circumventing the Terminal Control Area around Washington, and, from Annapolis, change course and head home. The flight would span three hundred fifty nautical miles, and would take, I figured roughly, five hours fifteen minutes, counting stops.

TUESDAY, SEPTEMBER 23RD.

It was still raining. I had done all the pre-flight planning I could do without having access to the weather briefings to compute the ground speeds and headings. I had decided to try the flight entirely by pilotage/dead reckoning, regardless of the omni stations that lay along the course. If I was going to make the trip, I might as well do it by the process of discovery.

WEDNESDAY, SEPTEMBER 24TH.

Still it rained. All local records for rainfall in September had long been broken. All local records for rainfall, any month, had now been passed. The rivers were in flood.

FRIDAY, SEPTEMBER 26TH.

Tom called and sounded very restless. There had been nothing for him to do all week at the airport, so he spent the time at home. It made him anxious.

SATURDAY, SEPTEMBER 27TH.

The rains stopped.

SUNDAY, SEPTEMBER 28TH.

Sunlight and the chirruping of birds, for the first time in eleven days.

MONDAY, SEPTEMBER 29TH.

Now my nerves were on edge. It made me anxious just to think of leaving home.

TUESDAY, SEPTEMBER 30TH

Today was it. I showed at the airport at nine a.m. The weather looked problematic. The storm system had not been blown clear by a high pressure center or swept away to sea by a cold front from the northwest; it had simply moved on, northeast, and the winds today were feed-back winds from the center of the low. Tom considered having me stand down and wait another day. Bill had his doubts too. I would be crossing the Blue Ridge at the four thousand foot summit. The air was thick with haze; moisture ridden. It would be worse at altitude. Bill suggested I call Martinsburg Flight Service Station. "They know the valley," he said, "They can tell you everything that's going to happen as far south as Roanoke."

I made the call. The briefer forecast five miles visibility before eleven a.m., with clouds scattered at five thousand, occasionally broken. Visibility would be unrestricted after eleven. That seemed to decide it. I would go.

Tom reviewed my nav. log and found an error in the computations. "Too much hurrying," I said.

"You only had a week," said Tom.

I checked out the Colt. Tom gave a hand in towing it out. An afterthought occurred to me, so I asked Tom for his advice. I had been concerned since charting this course about the military jet traffic that comes and goes from the many military bases along the coast. "Don't worry," said Tom, "You won't see anything." After that, I got to wondering what he meant.

At ten fifty-five, I started up the Colt. A minute later I was airborne, climbing out. I was going to shoot one practice landing to warm up.

I came around the approach turns power off and midway down final I perceived the slope to be marginally short. Another student pilot had just walked out of the hangar and was standing to one side of the runway to watch my landing. I was of a mind in that approach, whose point it was to make the runway on a glide, to try to stretch the glide. I thought I'd make it on. I saw it would be close. The Colt came in above the airport boundary, over hedges, over grass. The threshold of the runway lay before me, below the nose. The runway flattened out. Very low. I watched the threshold. It began to rise. Too low. I came back on the wheel regardless. The ship flared out. The wheels touched down, beautifully, in the grass.

While still in rotation, the nose gear up in the air, I felt the main gears bump over the lip of the runway and roll on hard surface. I thought I saw astonishment in the face of the other student pilot. I knew for sure what Tom would have to say. What's done was done I thought, so I put the power on and I was on my way, eleven o one a.m.

The Potomac was in flood. I crossed it near Poolesville and marveled at the sight of it, a gash four times its normal width, brown and roiling in visible turmoil. It lapped away at the land and devoured its own flood plain. My course from Leesburg was a straight line to Shenandoah Valley, two hundred and thirty degrees true. The straight-line distance between two points was a practical stratagem; it was the shortest distance. But, today, it was an error, poor tactics for the mountain crossing. The Colt was approaching the ridge line of the mountains at an angle of incidence with the ridge of twenty-five degrees. Better to cut straight across than narrow in at that close angle. It would keep me over the ridges longer, and at their highest elevations. Visibility was poor and deteriorating as the countryside beneath the airplane rose. I began to climb, forced up by the contours of the land.

I reached thirty-five hundred when I flew by Sperryville, the last checkpoint to the east of the mountains. The ridges lay to starboard, astern, abeam and ahead on the quarter. Peaks stood dead ahead and on the port quarter. I trimmed the Colt into one more climb, going up to forty-five hundred. Visibility forward was under five miles. The engine began to sound hollow, the mixture running rich at altitude. I advanced the throttle to keep up power in the climb.

At eleven forty-five, I was atop the first mountains. The Colt had reached altitude, yet the ridges seemed higher, the illusion of refraction. I had been through that before; even two weeks before I had seen what northeast winds could do to visibility when humid air banks up against a mountain range. The farther peaks looked even higher. Mountains were behind me, under me, ahead of me and on both sides, and they seemed to rise.

Visibility shrank, by the moment. The mountains took on aspects of the Confederate dead. They seemed daguerrotypes; immense figures caught in a frieze; surprised, loitering, in different poses as if snapped from ragged conversation, askance from one another. They were shrouds of mass. No mere resemblance existed between the chart and reality. One saw the ridge and it was real, imminent, and there. What was conceived at home was gone. The contour lines looked neat at home; the chart showed the mountains contained. Now, what I saw was peak after peak extending back to grey. There was no end to it. I broke course, turned west, cut over the saddle. Anything, any heading, like a bird, sweep and swoop, like a gull through the fog, through the mooring posts along the docks at dawn.

Down from the saddle visibility improved. Signs of the valley out ahead of me appeared. I held four thousand feet. To the left, south, southwest, more mountains stood. To the right, ahead I saw one town, golden in rarefied light. I turned the Colt to a heading of two forty. I did not wish to make, all over again, all the errors I had made at Carlisle. I saw the Shenandoah, shining in sunlight, rich as cocoa in its own wash. From the perspective of altitude, it seemed loosed from a coil, like a rope or a snake; winding back and forth to the south.

I tracked on the river, picking up checkpoints with railroad tracks that ran along the river and through the river's towns. Luray, Shenandoah, Elkton lay along the way. A highway ran along the railroad tracks, then crossed them and recrossed in a braid. I picked the patterns out and tracked. Above Elkton, I resected my original course and returned to my original heading. The final twenty miles went easily enough. I raised sight of the airport at a quarter after twelve.

I landed upwind on runway 04. The airport had a windsock but no T. The runway was a mile in length. When I turned off from the runway, a young man came out onto the service area and began signaling me with two semaphore flags. I had never seen those before, at least not directed at me, but the signals made sense, such as "Come this way," and "Turn to your right," and "Stop." I was grateful to the man for working at my level of communication. I shut down the Colt and got out.

"Want gas?" the man asked.

"Left tank," I said. "Would you sign my log book, too?"

He took my pen and wrote a scrawl in the book. "We use runway twenty-two for a calm wind runway," he remarked.

I looked at the windsock blowing fifty degrees. He looked too and went about his business pumping gas.

In the office where I paid the bill, the airport manager confronted me. "Your radio not working?" he inquired.

"It works," I said. We let it go at that.

Outside, I was back on hands and knees to review the log for the second leg southeast. The mountains from there appeared no more than hazy hills. They did not look imposing in the least, or even very high. It seemed I had been down on hands and knees in the service area of every airport I had visited so far.

At five minutes after one, I took off, downwind this time, as the management preferred. I circled back in a climb and turned to heading. The ridges where my course recrossed would be eight hundred feet lower than the elevation farther north. I could see why it took the settlers, the pioneers, so long to make the break through the gaps of the Blue Ridge; why the Shenandoah represented the western bound and long frontier for many years. The eastern plains were a comfort to be kept.

The recrossing went smoothly. Visibility increased. The sun worked in my favor now, for it shone from above and just behind the airplane. Charlottesville lay ahead, and Richmond beyond. I looked for Monticello, but missed it as I passed.

The piedmont levelled into plains. I occupied myself with course-keeping, pilotage and busy-work. The cockpit became my office, the long solitude of flight turned insular. There were times and distances, rates and numbers, gauges, pointers, needles, and, of course, the constant vigil on the sky. My head filled with a pleasant reverie of many voices, all of them my own, aspects of skills. I had a crew on board inside my mind; pilot, navigator, radio man and meteorologist, even a flight engineer. The simplest tasks took time. Time passed. It consoled me for the fact that I could not take a break, or leave my "desk."

The James River appeared, well above its banks. Now, I realized something that was nudging into thought since I had passed the Potomac and seen the Shenandoah. The rivers were the shaping force across the land. I had thought of them the other way, as passive, following terrain. But they shaped terrain. They forged it, gouged it out, deposited it downstream and ran. The rivers as much made the valley as took it as given as a course. So obvious from the air. The rivers were not neat now, they did not seem ribbon-like, in place. The rivers looked like gashes, and the countryside was scarred.

At home, I had conceived of this flight as a course reversing time. I thought of it in social terms, backtracking history from west to east, the Shenandoah to the settlements at Jamestown and Williamsburg. It would not run that way at all. The social course was not so clear. It passed too fast. The geologic course was what appeared. The shape of things, the land, the basis of the social past. The more I used the chart to match up what I saw, the more I considered that the airplane was not moving over land so much as the land was retrogressing beneath my point of view. One image and sequence eliding with another. I began to believe the land lay on a scroll; the chart could only tell me what must play past. For a distance I travelled in twenty minutes, Mr. Jefferson required a day. He made a stop. I moved ahead. He drank, he spoke with other men, he slept; he stabled his horse, he lodged himself, his boots were mired in mud. I moved, apart from that, persuaded by the scroll. He stood stock still on Monticello and took in the view; I passed without even seeing his handiwork of half a life, a minute of time in flight.

Below Richmond, I turned east. I-95 passed underneath the plane. The James reappeared to my left, grandly arrayed in its flood stage. The river bent southeasterly, while the Colt winged out above its waters. On gaining its northern bank, I looked ahead and saw Jamestown, the features of the island quite distinct. On the chart, chartmakers had marked it with a pin; that meant a checkpoint on a VFR approach, no more important to them, or to me in the air, than to the navigator of the ship in the year 1607, who thought it looked safe in a river of no name. From Jamestown, the airport lay three miles dead ahead.

At ten minutes to two, I was standing in the service area. This time, I decided to review my log inside. In the office, amidst a number of friendly and, for the most part, young people, I ate my lunch from a brown paper bag. I found I had no appetite. All I could think of as I ate was to get back in the Colt and fly. I even lost my desire for cigarettes. I had smoked none since I arrived at Davis so many hours before. It seemed a day. It seemed I had been riding that airplane seat forever. The soft cushion of the seat in the lounge was too soft. My body was bent to the shape of the Colt. An airplane hits a bump at a hundred miles an hour, and the air becomes hard. A long flight was harder than a long ride in a car. It amused me to think that it was easier than a long ride on a horse. My thighs weren't chafed.

At three thirty, I took off. I circled out over the river and came back across the airport on my heading, zero one four, still climbing to altitude. Colonial Williamsburg eased by below the right wing. It looked no different than any brickbuilt town I'd seen. Antiquity at rest.

WEDNESDAY, OCTOBER 1ST.

No flying.

FRIDAY, OCTOBER 3RD.

I called Tom at noon to ask if he wanted to go night flying again. He said no, rather that I should come out at my usual hour, three, and practice dead stick landings in the Colt.

* * *

Over the week-end, I grew impatient. I felt Tom was changing the rules on me in the middle of the game. He had assigned a new maneuver for me Friday, and told me I had to learn it if I wanted to proceed. I thought I was at the end of things to learn. The new maneuver raised the standards for what was acceptable in a landing. It was the accuracy landing, a term that involves a very special set of meanings. First of all, the landing was made at a designated point, called the one hundred eighty degree point. Second, it was made at a constant power setting, or with the power off in the case of a dead stick accuracy landing. Third, the rules allowed for the landing to be overshot by as much as two hundred feet beyond the 180 degree point, but they prohibited the landing from being undershot. The airplane had to touch down at least even with the one-hundred-eighty-degree point. And last, the glide must be flown at a constant airspeed.

On Friday, at Davis, I used runway 26, and Tom designated the windsock as the 180 degree point. The term, 180 degree point, meant that the glide proceeded through half a compass, one hundred eighty degrees. It began on the downwind leg, at a point even with the windsock, went through the two turns, to base and final, and came back upwind on final as far as the windsock again. Through the approach, I was to hold a power off glide with an airspeed of seventy. That the touchdowns Friday were seldom in the vicinity of the windsock came as no surprise to me. A landing that would have been triumphant in July would fail me now. The landings of August would no longer do. To get the airplane down, to get it down and on and safely was not enough. To bring it in dead stick, and to correct for a cross wind by holding a slip, even to make a one wheel landing and grease it on, all that was insufficient for me now. Like the angels in the Middle Ages, now I had to dance on the head of a pin.

TUESDAY, OCTOBER 7TH.

It was a fair day, winds light from the south, southwest. We went dual and Tom put me under the hood for forty minutes. I resented the review, but at the end of the time agreed I had been in need of it. We picked up on a review of ground reference maneuvers and did S-turns east along route 40. My inexperience with those turns showed up in sloppy execution. Tom was patient, but dissatisfied. At the intersection of State Route 97, near Tridelphia, we broke off and Tom introduced yet another ground reference maneuver, the Figure 8.

We flew over the intersection in line with Route 40, eastbound and seven hundred feet above the highway. Tom had me fix a point to the right on the state route, then roll into a turn to the right and fly a turn-about-the-point. We came out of the turn at our original position and immediately rolled to the left and repeated the maneuver to the north. The Figure 8 combined elements of an S-turn with elements of the turn-about-a-point to help me learn to cope with wind, although the wind aloft today was fairly light. We flew them north and south, then broke away and flew them east and west.

At the conclusion of maneuvers, we headed for the airport. I assumed I would begin working on accuracy landings again. Instead, however, Tom had me climb the airplane as we neared the airport until we flew over at twenty-five hundred feet. We checked the pattern below us, saw that it was clear, and Tom announced that I was to learn still another ground reference maneuver, the spiral glide. The purpose of this maneuver was to bring the airplane down from altitude while keeping it above one spot. It was to be used, as Tom explained, in case the engine quit and I was over the place I wanted to use to land.

Runway 26 was active. We were over the field to the south of the airport when he pulled the power back. The nose dropped, I cranked in trim, and rolled the airplane to the left to start the turn. Down we came, in a spiral. My actions grew quite hectic as we dropped. I watched the altimeter, watched the airspeed indicator, scanned the needle and ball. I watched the ground for reference to our track, watched out for other aircraft since the spiral brought us down directly on top of the downwind leg. I had to time the turns with the loss of altitude each turn to bring the ship out of the spiral at pattern altitude; one turn too many would be too low, one turn too few, too high. And coordinate the turns as in turns-about-a-point, to check against drift, to keep us in position for the downwind leg of the approach when we rolled out.

I got through the spiral, rolled out of it heading east at fourteen hundred feet, on the downwind leg of the pattern. I turned to base, then turned to final, and realized the slope was short. I had to add some power to make it reach. "That's miserable," said Tom.

Of course it was. When we taxied back, Tom said to stop. I stopped. He climbed out. It was unforgivable to start a glide with nineteen hundred feet to kill, then come in short. Tom looked at me. "Are you going to fly any more?"

"You mean today?"

"I mean right now."

I gave him my best face: enthusiastically half assed.

WEDNESDAY, OCTOBER 8TH.

The weather continued warm and hazy with light southerly winds. Autumn had not bitten us so far. Tom sent me out solo to review ground reference maneuvers and work on accuracy landings again. I took the Colt north to Route 40 and began S-turns. The crews were out again, working at the construction sites. I used the yellow barrels as I had the times before for reference to the centers of the turns. The Colt snaked over the sites along the road, back and forth, north and south, gradually winding eastward from Mount Airy. Banking, unbanking, banking, unbanking; the highway went by, the highway came round, crossed and recrossed. I looked at boards and rails and mounds of dirt, at trucks and barrels and men with picks and men with air hammers. The crews looked up. The Colt went by. The crews looked down. The ship came back again. I had the tingling feeling in the nape of my neck that if some of those guys had guns... Though then again, if I had bombs....

I broke off, flew back to Davis, and climbed to twenty-five hundred. I checked the pattern, nine hundred feet below, then pulled the power to start the spiral glide. Down came the Colt, tobogganing around; two thousand, eighteen hundred, seventeen, four hundred feet a turn. Two times around, I rolled out on downwind. At sixteen hundred feet I had altitude to spare. From there, I set up the approach, still gliding, for an accuracy landing on runway 26. I slowed the airspeed down to seventy, took the downwind leg out over the road to Laytonsville, and made the turn to base. I had a determination not to come in short, and realized, on base, the slope was far too high. I finagled the altitude away as best I could. I bellied the base leg deeper, turned wide, turned late; came over the Paille's back yard, directly over the top of their willow tree; any move to waste the distance of the glide, and then the slip, to kill the lift. The ship came down, racing. I swerved back to the left, the left wing down, deep in the slip.

The windsock sailed by. I levelled out the wings as the ship regained the runway's centerline at last, and then flared out with the runway halfway gone.

I made the landing touch and go, climbed back to altitude and tried it all again.

One touchdown later, six hundred feet too long, I put the power on again and climbed to make an exit from the pattern. I flew back to Route 40 and started Figure 8s at our intersection. The third time around, a woman came out from the front door of her house and stood on the steps of the porch to watch the plane. She seemed to disapprove.

FRIDAY, OCTOBER 10TH.

It rained. Tom called in the afternoon. I told him I was doing poorly because I didn't feel resistance; it had all become routine. It interested him that I confused resistance with goals. He mentioned that a private pilot's license did not mean that you knew how to fly; only that you were licensed and could begin to learn. The real learning, Tom said, occurred in the two hundred to three hundred hours you put in after the license. I said I was ready to take my test. Tom was genuinely surprised, not merely at the prospect that I'd flunk. He told me that, come Tuesday, I would get a sneak preview.

Tuesday, October 14th.

The weather was fair; the winds blustering from the southwest. The air was full of bumps. "Get the hood," said Tom.

We started up the engine at ten past ten. On the exit from the pattern, I turned north. Without Tom's asking me, I began to do Dutch Rolls. I did a dozen beautifully; it made Tom laugh. "Okay," he said, "Now give me a left turn to three six zero degrees. Hold eighteen hundred feet. Hold forty-five degrees of bank."

I checked traffic and rolled the Colt over in the bank. I fed in rudder, checked the marker on the attitude gyro and held forty-five. I came back on the wheel and held back-pressure; watched the ball for signs of slip or skid, and eased off the rudder. I watched the altitude.

I watched the horizon, tilted diagonally, slicing the windshield. I watched the attitude gyro. Around we went. I watched the directional gyro. The headings brushed by. One eighty, one sixty, one forty, one twenty, one hundred. Eighteen hundred, altitude. Heading markers eighty, sixty, forty. I started rolling out. Check the ball. Check the heading. Time the roll-out with the heading. Check the altitude and relax back-pressure on the wheel. Twenty-five, twenty, fifteen, ten. The rate of turn decreased. The horizon returned to its horizontal plane. Five, three, one; level; three-sixty. "Good," said Tom, "Now one to the right."

At the end of the turns, we started S-turns. Route 40 lay ahead. I pulled the power back. The Colt dropped to fourteen hundred. I added power again and levelled out. We zipped over, heading north and banked to right. I spotted off a barrel. The turn came round. I fiddled with the trim, the throttle, the pressure on the wheel. The ship began to climb. I crossed southbound and overbanked the turn. The ship began to slip. "Too nervous," said Tom, "Relax." He scored the maneuver on a pocket notebook. The third time across, I relaxed, and the fourth time across, I improved.

"Okay," said Tom, "Some Figure 8s."

No break. Not a second between one maneuver and the next. We overflew the junction of the state route and Route 40. I rolled the Colt into a bank to right and started coming round. The wind was strong, buffeting the ship, upsetting the banks, disrupting the turns. Bank to right, roll out, re-roll and bank to left. The track described infinity signs above the crossing roads. We broke away and circled back. I flew them north and south. "That's good," said Tom. He marked his book. "Now put on the hood."

I took an extra five seconds to fit the hood on my head. It was my breather.

"Fly me to Westminster now," said Tom.

I turned to a northerly heading and trimmed the ship to climb. I tuned the omni in. Vibrations buzzed inside the hood. The wind intruded on my world of instruments today. We were rafting, canoe-ing on the Shenandoah, we were running rapids in our boat today.

This was the roughest wind, the bumpiest air I had flown in so far. Instead of smoothing out at altitude, it just grew worse. The chop got heavier. The drift became tenacious. Course keeping was an estimate at best. I hacked off headings, watched the needles dance. We climbed, we dipped, we sank outright; retrimmed and climbed again and slued around. The omni's needle wavered and deflected and I changed the course to track it down, then overshot and watched it swing the other way. The ship slammed and banged and bumped around. We hit one patch of satin air, a contrast so total and abrupt I held my breath. Three seconds later, back in chop.

"Over the station," I yelled.

"Okay," yelled Tom, "Now turn and track to Frederick."

I turned the ship and tracked outbound. No break. No let up. I heard Tom's voice interrupting my contentions. I resented it. I pushed the sound away. I shut it out.

"Climb to twenty-one hundred," he yelled.

Why? I wanted to press on; my reflexes had momentum of their own. Dogged. Fight the rocks. Fight the rocky field. Plow ahead.

"Make a turn to the left to one eight zero."

Reluctantly, I climbed and banked into the turn, abandoning the way to Frederick.

"Okay," said Tom.

One eight zero came round on the gyro. Twenty-one hundred at the hands of the altimeter.

"Hold seventy miles an hour," he said, "And give me a turn to the right to zero nine zero degrees."

Yes? Yes? What else?

"And descend to sixteen hundred feet," he said.

Worked so hard to get there, then came down.

"Take off the hood," said Tom.

I took it off. The light was blindingly bright. I looked around outside in glare. Route 40 passed underneath the plane.

"See that field," said Tom, pointing off the nose. "Rectangular courses to the right."

No break. No pause. From the hood and the instruments to the field and ground references again. I flew along the field fence, picked up the drift and correction for the wind, snapped off a turn to right and ran the field line north. I snapped another turn and squared it off. I ran the field line east and hugged the fence. I squared the downwind turn. "That's good," said Tom. "Now left."

I circled out and came back running left.

"Let's find another field," said Tom, "And find a bush for turns-about-a-point."

No hitch. No let up. Tom scribbled in his book. How 'bout a cup of coffee, Tom? We scooted back across Route 40, heading north.

"There's a bush," said Tom. I pretended not to see it. He pointed again and made me look. A bush, a tiny shrub, a colorful little thing that somehow grew on the dome of a piebald field, surrounded by large neighbors, spruce and pine. At fifteen hundred feet, I made a right hand entry for the turns. I missed the entry, entered crosswind and drifted to the right until I lost sight of bush beneath the right wing. I rolled the Colt over to a bank of fifty degrees and looked out, down from Tom's window for the bush, one among thousands I could see. We were flying over woods. I had lost the field, too.

"Try it to the left," said Tom.

I rolled the ship the other way. The field and bush appeared.

Tom made an entry in his notebook. I broke away and flew upwind, then turned and charged the bush again. I made the turns to right and broke away again and circled back. I flew them to the left.

"Head south," said Tom.

We crossed Route 40, heading south. A break for lunch at last? No. Tom reached in front of me and pulled the throttle out. The engine lopped off to an idle. The ship began to glide. "Is the test like this?" I asked.

"Oh no," said Tom, "It's hard."

WEDNESDAY, OCTOBER 15TH

The weather was very fair today; the winds persisted from the southwest. I went flying in the Colt, alone, to review right-hand entries to ground reference maneuvers, and to practice course keeping on the omni. Neither of those things was uppermost in mind, however. Autumn had arrived, and the countryside was brilliant in its light. The Colt swept over the knolls and bluffs and woods around Westminster. Each new heading brought new views. The woodlands seemed like seas, the crowns of trees like limitless realm. Fields were lined in barberry red. I felt as if I were sailing. The sky was cloudless. I could descend from it and rise again at will. So free, the morning was my own. It had happened overnight.

I was extremely fortunate to have had this opportunity, and knew it. How very improbable it was. How far one's course tracks and retracks back around upon itself, and goes from here to there, this morning to another week, through one escape and through another, in and out of windfalls, around the edge of failures, to arrive at surprise. Here, in this time, you are free. More humble than that, it is you and an airplane, alone in the sky.

FRIDAY, OCTOBER 17TH.

The weather had changed. Tom and I were waiting for an opportune occasion to go night flying again.

TUESDAY, OCTOBER 21ST.

Tonight was it. Orville and Tom were the only ones left at the airport when I arrived. It was early, but completely dark. The six weeks that had passed since the first night flying I had done with Tom were more than weeks that shortened days. They deepened nights. It had been years since I associated Halloween, or late October, with spookiness at night, but the association came back in those moments I stood outside the hangar there tonight. The wind came from the south and swelled. It rose and fell, and sounded like surf in the hardwood trees. The air was thick, had grain and pebbly texture, as coarse as wood!

191

I looked around at the airport. All the surfaces were encompassed in an active dark. It unnerved me. I made no bones in saying so to Tom. He made no bones in looking grim. Orville, who was ready to go home, changed his mind and decided he would stay.

"Let's get it over with," said Tom. I went to get my flashlight from the car. Neither of us said another word and the tension between the two of us communicated a war of nerves.

I rolled the Colt out onto runway 26. The twinkly rows of lights lay out ahead. I put the power on and we charged down the dark between the rows. The cross wind grabbed us at the take-off point. I felt the wheels sidle on the runway as the weight on them decreased. On the climb-out, I crabbed left, fifteen degrees to correct for wind. The darkness seemed nearly blue or bruise, so deep. Every light below was ringed with a violet sheen.

The first approach, I came in high and wobbly, drifting to the right in the wind. Gravel spit out beneath the right wing the instant we touched down. The wheel rolled in grass. I had landed half on, half off the runway in the dark. I kept us down and brought us back in line. I could hear Tom wheeze and then relax, sit back. We rolled out to a stop, then taxied back and went again.

The second time around, I improved the track against the wind. We came down final fast, landed long and landed fast. We rolled out long and stopped. Every pore of my body had opened up. I was covered in sweat. The cockpit smelled of fear. Tom sat back, exhaling audibly again. My exhale matched his own. I was one hundred per cent tonight. Every thought of my mind gathered to the point of one thought: land.

We taxied back and went again. Around the pattern, down the long approach. On final, Tom asked if he could do this landing. I never answered back. I just meant no. He didn't take the ship from me; I didn't give it up. The runway lights began to spread. The hangar strobe flashed by. I swung the heading around to true. The nose came up. I rushed to full rotation and we stalled. The nose began rotating down again; I reached to add the power but we hit the runway first.

The ship stayed on and we rolled out to a stop. "Do you mind if I land the airplane once?" asked Tom.

"No, go right ahead," I said, "Go right ahead."

Tom handled the ship as we taxied back. We taxied up to the runway, entered, turned and rolled. He took off smoothly and we climbed to pattern altitude. I sat back and felt the coolness of the air against my forehead. Tom made his turn to downwind and flew a straight row on the downwind leg. He corrected niftily for wind. He pulled the power back, then cranked in trim. We tracked on out and turned to base. I watched the airport's lights begin to come around.

On final, Tom worked the engine down, shading the adjustments of power and slope. It was a fine approach. He corrected for the turbulence, crabbed against the drift. The hangar strobe flicked past. We were sinking. The first two runway lights swept by; still sinking. He swung the ship around fifteen degrees, truing our heading with the direction of travel. The drift set in. We drifted to the right. The second two lights swept by. Still too high. Tom pulled the flare regardless. The ship whooshed out, rotating, then it dropped. We landed off the runway to the right. The impact sent a Whammo through my ears.

We taxied back and quit. I shut the Colt down. Orville greeted us with laughter. "What's the matter, boys?"

"Did you see that last landing?" asked Tom.

"I sure did," Orville said, "'It liked to stood my hair on end.'"

WEDNESDAY, OCTOBER 22ND.

Within twelve hours the world reverted. October shone again. A cold front had passed at four a.m. At nine, the winds were from the north, northwest and strong.

Tom was looking very glum. I asked him what the matter was. He said he was up until three a.m. He sent me in the office for the hood.

As soon as we were airborne, I went on instruments and completed the climb-out. We headed north and began precision turns, then turns with climbs and descents, then stalls.

"That's good," said Tom, "Fly me to Westminster." I tuned Westminster, identified the code, centered on a radial and tracked. The wind was quartering from ahead and from the left. I crabbed against the wind as much by reflex as by thought. The course kept true.

"Take off the hood," said Tom.

I lifted off the hood. He was grading me again, reviewing last week's errors.

"Go find the bush," he said.

Route 40 passed below. I recognized the field ahead and found the bush. I entered cross wind and flew the turns to right. It did not matter now whether that maneuver began downwind; I flew it with a skill if not a grace, because I knew the ship.

Three times around. "Just fine," said Tom, "Now take me back."

I headed south and, when we reached the airport, Tom asked for an accuracy landing. I shot it, came in long but smooth, and held the slip right through the end. "Go again," said Tom.

I put the power on. The Colt climbed back to pattern altitude. The second time around I made the same misjudgment of the slope and overshot the windsock by four hundred feet. We rolled out to a stop. "You try it now," I said to Tom.

Tom laughed.

"Come on," I said, "I want to see you make an accuracy landing."

"Okay," said Tom and took the controls away from me. We taxied back and entered the runway. Tom put the power on and we took off. At the windsock on the downwind leg, he pulled the power off. I watched the airspeed as he made his glide and noted where he made his turns. He made the turns in the same places I made mine, but he flew the downwind leg, and base, and turn to final holding eighty. The faster airspeed produced a faster sink, and we came in final low and fast. He rolled the ship just slightly to the right, and played back with a yaw to left. "Just play the slip and you can bleed off airspeed," he said. I watched the speed come down; he had traded speed for stretch. We came in low, beneath the brunt of the wind, skimmed over the shrubs at the airport's boundary and essentially flew in ground effect until we reached the flare. The wheels touched down thirty feet beyond the windsock. "How's that?" asked Tom.

"It's very good," I answered.

"It's perfect," he replied.

The roll-out finished with half the runway left. We taxied back. At the hold-short line we stopped. Tom set the parking brake and opened up the door. "That's all for me," he said. "You're on your own. I'm going to sign you off today. Fly some more if you want. We'll fill out the forms in the office when you're done. After that, you can take your test any time you set up an appointment with an examiner."

"Hey, just a second," I said, when his words sank in. "I'm through?"

"All through."

"What about the accuracy landings?"

"Work on them. You should."

"But won't they fail me on the test?"

"You won't be taking a commercial pilot's test."

* * *

The private pilot's test consisted of a short flight, much like the test drive one takes to get a driver's license. The student shows up at the hour of appointment at the airport where the examiner operates. The student provides the airplane, and presents the examiner with a record of his or her activities as a student, plus the endorsement of the flight instructor.

Bill and Tom both recommended that I choose the examiner from Easton Airport, a man named Newnam. Mr. Newnam had passed on Tom for Tom's licenses, and he was a friend of Bill's. Bill spoke of him as being fair minded and commonsensical. "He can tell in about a minute," said Bill., "Whether you've got it or not."

I made the appointment Wednesday afternoon, for Tuesday,

October 28th., eleven a.m. Throughout the remainder of the week, I felt I was in limbo. Tom's endorsement came on the bottom line of a tally sheet listing activities I had completed over the past ten months. They included not only ground school and the FAA written exam, but also all the flight activities and the hours in each activity. I had amassed ninety-seven hours and fifteen minutes total time in airplanes. Thirty-five of those hours had been solo. Over ten of those hours were solo cross country. Five hours went to instrument flight, and three hours to flying at night. Not on the record·were the two hundred and twenty landings I had made, or the several I had not.

I mused on an association I had formed. I had begun to think of this man, Mr. Newnan, as a greybeard, gaunt, tall and lanky, low-voiced and rather rough-boned, angular sort of soul. As the hour grew nearer, I realized why it was I thought of him that way. It was because his name associated with HIGH NOON, the film, and my anxiety associated the Western myth of confrontation with properties of Gary Cooper in the lead.

TUESDAY, OCTOBER 28TH.

Easton Airport lies southeast of Davis, sixty-five miles. It is a fairly large airport, a mile from the town of Easton, on Maryland's Eastern Shore.

The weather today was foul. The weather forecasters were lying. They had said clear, they had said scattered, four thousand, and visibility five or visibility eight. All that was nonsense. The sky was full of webby clouds. The clouds were refracting and diffusing sunlight into a cauldron's mix of different greys. Greys and tans, brash sandy, tawny duns, coppers, bronzes, anything but bright and blue. There were bands and straps of clouds a thousand feet above the ground, a layer of haze above that, and banks of cumulus clouds above that. It was a warm day, the winds were light, southerly, southwest, the air exceedingly moist.

"I've seen this weather before," said Tom.

"What do you think?" I asked.

"I think you should cancel. It'll be worse when you fly across the bay."

I waited it out. I paced in the office, went outside frequently and checked the sky, went into the hangar and paced in the hangar.

"Got everything ready?" Mina asked.

"Everything's ready."

"Got the hood?"

"I put it in the plane."

"Got your tally sheet?"

"Yes."

"Got your log book?"

"Yes."

"Got your FCC permit?"

"Yes."

"Got your student pilot's license?" cracked Tom.

I continued pacing.

"I still think you should call and cancel for today," Tom said a moment later. He went over to the corner of the hangar and filled a bucket of water. When he returned, he began swabbing down the Colt, cleaning the bugs off the prop. and the wings. I walked outside and checked the sky again.

"Why not call over to Easton," suggested Bill. "Call and find out what their weather is."

I went back into the office and placed the call. An assistant who worked with Mr. Newnam answered and told me they were VFR, with clear skies and good visibility. "They must be in another world," I said to Bill.

"Well, wait until the very last minute," he said, "Then you can make up your mind. It'll take you forty minutes to get there. You can leave at ten twenty and still get there on time. Just take off, turn right onto your heading and go."

Tom finished swabbing down the Colt. The ship looked good. I thanked him for his concern. He had been noticeably quiet most of the morning. Concern it was.

Ten twenty came and went. The sun broke through and, for a moment, shone. "I think I'll try," I said.

No one said no, so I pulled the Colt out onto the grass, looked back at the three forlorn faces, Mina, Tom, and Bill, and climbed aboard.

At ten twenty three the Colt took off. I turned to heading and stayed below the clouds. The air was full of bump and chop, unstable; the estimate of light winds pertained to surface winds, not winds aloft. The farther east I went, nearing the bay, the lower the bases of the clouds dropped. At Woodland Beach, sea level, I was down to sixteen hundred feet. Visibility had not once exceeded three miles; intermittently, it shrank to two. Now, it stayed at two. I headed out across the Chesapeake. The waters of the bay were dead as slate. The clouds had no border, no margins, no markings; they gobbed out into the air, or the air accumulated in them, without distinction of the two.

I held heading. No more horizon appeared. One shade of grey contrasted with a dozen shades of grey. There was no upward visibility, no sign of sky, no sun, just layers and tangling swaths of different densities of grey.

The air became quite smooth. I picked up the coast of Kent Island. The pilotage points fell in place. I was on course. The island's coast receded behind the plane. I was surprised that visibility still held at two miles.

The Colt surged on across the bay again; four miles ahead would lie the Eastern Shore. Midway in the span, the clouds began to sandwich me. I entered a cloud mass without realizing I had entered until all slant range visibility was gone. I pulled the power back. The Colt dropped. At nine hundred feet, I came out from the bottom of the cloud and saw the bay again. I levelled out, looked down. Suddenly, the bay disappeared.

I went on instruments and turned the Colt around.

Within a moment, Kent Island reappeared. Something caught my eye out the right side window. I turned my head. An Air Force F-80, all white, came out of the cloud bank to the right of me and passed astern. It missed me by a hundred yards. I looked to the left. It re-entered the cloud and was gone. I looked back to the right, as if I knew. The wingman came out of the cloud and crossed my stern. I watched him enter the cloud. There had been no sound. It took about a second for each one. I thought they looked like sharks.

* * *

I went back into limbo for the rest of the week. I called Easton from Davis and made another appointment, for Wednesday, November 5th., eleven a.m. again. Tom pointed out I could have radioed the request in from the ship. I told him I had other things in mind.

By Monday, I decided I needed to practice more. I called Tom. We made a date for Tuesday morning, same old time. "What do you want to do?" asked Tom.

"I'd like to fly on instruments again."

WEDNESDAY, NOVEMBER 5TH.

I was blessed with sleep.

I woke before daybreak and called the Washington Flight Service Station. The briefer read the forecast for eleven a.m. Winds, three-twenty at nineteen knots, at three thousand feet. The forecast for Baltimore, clear. I made out my log and left for the airport.

At nine thirty, I was ready to go. The Colt was on the line, checked out. "What's the rush?" asked Tom.

"No rush." I stopped rushing and paced around the apron for a while. At nine forty-five, I told Tom I had to get started, even if only to fly turns-about-a-point.

"Okay," Tom said, "But one thing. One piece of advice, that's all I have to give to you."

I nodded yes.

"Newnam is going to pull the power on you. It'll happen when you're making your approach."

"All right."

"Don't come in short." Tom shook my hand. He wished me luck. We said good-bye. We had both given this whole business our best shots.

At nine fifty, I took off in the Colt. It was a cross wind take-off. I assumed I would not have the problem of a cross wind at Easton. One of their runways was runway 32, directly into the wind.

Over the bay today, visibility was good. The winds aloft were steady, the air somewhat hazy but stable. The forecast had been accurate. I picked up the coast of the Eastern Shore, and within a few moments saw the airport. Easton was the largest airport I had been to. It had two abutting runways of four thousand feet, with bearings 32 and 14 reciprocal for one of them, 22 and 04 reciprocal for the other. Runway 32 was active. I made a power off approach. The Colt touched down with two-thirds of a mile of runway left. It took nearly five minutes to taxi to the service area.

I parked among distinguished ships, including several twins. I saw only one other person in the area, but I felt certain he was the man I was looking for. He stood next to the cabin of a blue and white Cessna. He had been watching me as I taxied up. He watched me turn around and park. When I climbed out, he nodded hello. He was about fifty-five years old and about six feet tall. He had a prominent adam's apple and an angular, raw-boned, leathery look. He was smiling. "You're all ready to go, aren't you?" he said.

I thought it was rather neat that Mr. Newnam had watched me land and taxi in. And come to think of it, I was feeling pretty much on top of things. "Yes sir," I said, "I am."

"I'll be right back," he said, and climbed aboard his airplane. I figured he had work to do. Who knew what flight examiners did? He had to check out a plane or go park it somewhere. I sat down on the wheel and waited. He started up the engine and taxied away.

Ten minutes later, he hadn't returned. I had to go to the bathroom. I went inside the main building and asked directions. When I came back, a man sitting at a desk in the office rose and spoke to me. "Are you here for your private pilot's test?" he asked.

"I am," I replied.

"Well, you better come here," he said.

"Mr. Newnam said to wait outside," I said.

"Mr. Newnan said come here," said Mr. Newnam.

Mr. Newnam was a very short man, perhaps in his fifties, with a young-looking, pudgy face. His manner of dress was very trim, and his voice soft, and softly restrained and clipped. He wore his hair brush-cut, a flat top from an earlier era. There wasn't so much as a whit of nonsense in his style.

He looked at my credentials, took my various documents and had me fill out forms. Moment by moment, my memory deteriorated. I had trouble with my address and my age.

When we got outside, we headed for the plane. I climbed aboard, and Mr. Newnam climbed in behind me. I felt a need to say something sociable. "Not much room in here," I said.

Several things were becoming very clear to me by the time I finished my inanity. Number one, the man was here to see me fly the plane, and number two, I was getting in my own way. Number one, I think my style of slapstick threw him off. Or I could say, my beard, my mustache, and my chipped tooth grin, but, whatever, I came on wrong to him. And that was my way of coping with the stress. I was ready to go nuts. I did the check list and kept hearing Bill's words, that Mr. Newnam would know in a minute if I could handle the plane. The check list was a way to show what I knew; reach surely and by reflex for every control switch and knob in the cockpit. If you have to think about what's next, or where to find it, then you might as well be through.

My hands did fine. The Colt started up. I checked the time, the oil pressure and gyros. We were ready to go. Instead, I launched into the run-up test. This was wrong. Mr. Newnam wasted no time in telling me it was wrong. It posed a discourtesy for people in the area, because of engine noise and prop. blast. And I had done it in spite of knowing better. Clearly, my own excitability had the best of me. I was doing myself in. I apologized, and, by that, conveyed at least my sense to him that I was human, too. The last thing I wanted was to contend for his authority. He thought I felt I knew a lot.

We taxied off to the left, not heading for runway 32, which lay in the other direction. Since we were heading for runway 22, I made an assumption that we were going to taxi on runway 22, an inactive runway, to get to runway 32, which it joined. We came to the end of the taxi strip and I rolled right by the hold-short line and almost onto the run-way. Something in the back of my mind said, "Stop, my man, or it's your ass." I stopped. Mr. Newnam was vexed, right to the point, I think, that if I said one thing in defense of what I was doing, he would tell me to turn around and go back to the service area, and that would be it. To the brink. Not off the ground.

We weren't going to use runway 32. We were going to use runway 22. He wanted a cross wind take-off in the Colt.

I did the run-up, and we went.

Mr. Newnam watched every move I made until we cleared the ground. And then, I think he sensed I felt relieved, because, in fact, I was extremely glad to have that airplane in the air. I tracked out along the runway's centerline, climbing and crabbing into the wind. We reached four hundred feet and I made the turn. He took over and flew the ship southwest. We passed Easton and the Choptank River. He asked me to put on the hood, and I put it on. He told me to take my time, and I did. I reached for the chart. He said I wouldn't need it right now. Then, I took over, on instruments.

We flew precision turns. His manner became much less abrupt with me; in fact, no longer abrupt but rather kind. We both, perhaps, were relieved of our misgivings. I answered his requests with "yes sir," and "okay." He told me I was flying well.

"Make a turn to the left to ninety degrees and climb to two thousand three hundred feet," he said.

I put the power on and began the climb, trimmed the ship and initiated the turn, rolled out of the turn and held the climb, then levelled out.

"Continue to fly at seventy miles an hour," he said.

I held seventy. He asked for the controls again. I sat and looked down at my lap. He put the ship through unusual attitudes. I waited for the shocks and jolts. They never came. I waited for the sashaying veers and yaws, but none occurred.

"Take over now," he said.

I looked up at the attitude gyro. The little airplane was banked slightly to the right below the bar. I corrected the Colt.

"Your correction was a little too rough," he said.

We tried again. I waited through the nudges and contrariety of motion. He returned the controls to me. I looked up and caught the little airplane over the bar, with the airspeed low, the ship near a stall. I let down the nose and fed in power, but again he noted I was rough.

He asked me to execute a stall. My roughness emerged full force. I rode the nose up and we broke cleanly and went over. Down we rushed and I recovered, with a loss of a hundred twenty feet.

"You let the nose down too far on the recovery," Mr. Newnam said. "Also, you're still rough."

I tried a second stall and broke it off very gently. Again I let the nose down in a rush to recover.

"You need only lose fifty feet in the recovery from a stall," he said. "Should you be on an approach some time and only a hundred feet above the ground, then what will you do if you stall?"

"Recover in fifty feet," I said.

"Precisely. Try it once without the hood."

I removed the hood and flew a turning stall out of a turn to the left, using fifteen hundred r.p.m. The best I could do was recover it in eighty. Again, I was rough.

"A nice airplane like this, well-behaved, stable as it is, you don't have to fly it so rough."

He took over to demonstrate his point. He flew the Colt the way he spoke of it, civilly. He coaxed it through moves, with next to no motion of his own. The ship responded, right on cue.

Mr. Newnam asked that I look up Salisbury Omni on my chart. Again, he told me to take my time, relax. While I looked for the station, he continued to fly the plane. I was so used to doing the two things at once that it disturbed me to have two hands free instead of one, and undivided time to see the chart. He told me to tune the omni in. As I did that, he continued to fly the plane. I identified the code and set up the omni bearing display so that the flag showed "To" and the needle centered. He gave me back the ship. I turned to heading, which took ten seconds, estimated an angle for wind correction, which used another five seconds, and then set out to track, another ten seconds, to total twenty-five, and he took the ship away again. "That's good," he said, "Sit back. Relax."

A moment later the airport came in view. Beneath the left wing, the town of Easton passed by. The air was delightfully smooth. Mr. Newnam entered the pattern for a left hand approach to runway 22. It was not entirely air that made the flight so smooth. The man flew the downwind leg in a perfect line.

"I'm going to cut the power off," he said. "I want you to fly the approach."

I nodded my head and looked down at the runway to our left.

"You may use all of the runway that you need for the landing," he continued, "But I require that you make it to the runway on the glide. Do you understand?"

"Yes sir."

He reached to the throttle and pulled the power off.

I rode out downwind and trimmed the ship to hold eighty. I cut the downwind leg short, and rolled into the turn to base. I saw the base leg would bring me in too high and so I bellied it out to add distance to the track. We flew into the wind on base; I turned to final and we had now a cross wind from the right. I put the ship into a slip. We came down in a hurry, tracking dead down the centerline of the runway. I looked out over the hood. The ship said flare. I pulled the wheel, saw details of the tarmac rise, and walked it on, right wheel first.

It was a long taxi to reach the taxi turn. "Son, that was a fine landing," Mr. Newnam said. He was looking at me, at <u>me</u>, for the first time since I had come there. "I didn't know you. I had never flown with you before." I looked at him as he spoke. We still had a way to go before we turned off the runway. We were just putting along now at five miles an hour. "I've had students come in here for tests," he said, "And a little wind like today's blows them right off the runway into the marsh."

"Okay," I said, "I've been through this before."

GLOSSARY

The following terms pertain to landing an airplane.

To flare out, the most important of the terms, means to rotate an airplane nose high, taking advantage of the cushioning effect of air near the runway, until the airplane has induced so much drag that it cannot fly slower, while at the same time so much lift that it cannot continue to descend. When the flare out is complete, the airplane will stall. If the stall occurs when the wheels of the airplane are one inch above the runway, you have the makings of a lovely landing.

The stall is the act of an airplane ceasing to fly.

Flying it into the runway describes a situation whereby the airplane makes contact with the runway before the flare out has been established. The term is known also by the euphemism, controlled crash.

To cut through ground effect is the precedent condition to flying it into the runway. Ground effect is the cushioning air provides an airplane near the surface of the runway. An airplane whose glide slope is too steep relative to the plane of the runway cuts through such cushioning. Tardiness on the part of the pilot in coming back on the stick, which produces rotation for the flare, is a typical cause, typically in combination with too low an airspeed, with its attendant steep slope and momentum downward. An airplane tends to carry on in its original direction of travel - the glide slope - at its original rate of travel - the approach speed. It is the flare out that alters that inertia.

Back-pressure, or to hold back-pressure, increase back-pressure (or let it off), or to come back on the stick (or control wheel), all pertain to that action on the part of the pilot to pull the stick or wheel toward him or her. The action translates mechanically into an upward deflection of the airplane's elevators, and so produces rotational pitch, nose up. The effects are to slow the airplane, to convert speed into lift, to induce drag. The term is pronounced as one word, "backpressure," on the first syllable.

To fly it onto the runway differs from flying it into the runway by more than the distinction of its preposition. This skilled maneuver requires the pilot to land the airplane at faster than stall speed, before the completion of a full flare out. The principle at hand is to convert into lift only that portion of flying speed necessary to retard descent during the last few feet to the runway, and so insure a smooth touch down. Since the airplane, so landed, continues to roll at a speed sufficient for flight, it remains for the pilot to keep the airplane down.

Balloon back up describes the premature conversion of airspeed to lift, with the effect that, if the airplane has landed, it takes off again, or, if the airplane is the process of flaring out, it begins, temporarily, to climb.

To hang it. To convert airspeed into lift at an excessive rate, thereby to complete the flare out while at an altitude one to eight feet above the runway.

To pancake indicates a fall to the runway from three to eight feet while the airplane is in a stalled condition.

To bounce it is to suffer multiple points of touchdown, typically the result of hanging it, flying it into the runway, or ballooning back up. Bouncing it differs from pancaking in that it is less drastic, very common, and occurs at the end of a drop that, as a rule, does not exceed three feet.

The glide slope, or glide path, describes the profile of an airplane's descent, from pattern altitude to the runway, in terms of altitude lost per forward distance travelled.

The roll out, marks the retardation of an airplane after it is groundborne.

To come in short denotes a routine expectation that the airplane will touch down in the first third of the runway. The term may be used in special contexts, however, to indicate an approach that is short of the runway. The term allies with to land short, to touch down short.

To land long refers to a landing in the middle third of the runway, and allies with the phrase, to come in high, which refers to the glide slope. Landing long may be emphasized in special contexts to mean landing too long, overrunning the runway, or, as the euphemism has it, running out of real state.

To slip, or to do a slip, pertains to cross-controlling an airplane by pitting ailerons against rudder. The contrary actions reduce lift very sharply and bring the airplane down. On a high approach, a slip is used to dump or kill altitude. On an approach during a cross wind, it is used to compensate for drift by slipping into the wind. As a rule, the slip is employed with back-pressure as well, either to avoid an increase in airspeed during the drop, or, in the case of a high, fast approach, to reduce the airspeed while steepening the slope.

To bleed off airspeed refers to a technique to extend a low, fast approach. In general, it means to rotate an airplane nose high, gradually, with respect to the glide slope, in order to trade flying speed for lift.

Holding an airspeed is standard practice in an approach and is accomplished by letting off back-pressure (and sometimes adding power) should the airspeed fall below a given mark, or coming back on the stick (and/or reducing power) should the airspeed start to rise.

To add power refers to the thrust of the engine and serves to extend the slope. Adding power while holding an airspeed insures that the power will be converted into lift.

To pull the power means to pull the throttle out, reducing the engine to idle. An approach, so flown, is considered dead stick.

The landing pattern, traffic pattern, or pattern is the route about an airport an airplane enters and flies in order to land. Pattern information involves a body of terms pertinent to organizing the route. Such information includes the active runway, which is to be used for the landing or take-off, the wind strength and direction, available by means of a wind sock that is visible from the air, and the direction, left or right, that turns are to be made in the approach to, or take-off from the given active runway. Unless otherwise noted, such turns are made to the left. Exceptions to this are indicated by the segmented circle, also visible from the air. The wind T and the tetrahedron are devices that indicate to a pilot which runway is active.

Unless otherwise noted, a complete circuit of the pattern, from an entry onto the active runway prior to a take-off to a roll out on that same runway following a landing, would include the following steps. 1. Entry onto the active runway. 2. The take-off roll. 3. The take-off. 4. The climb-out, using an imaginary extension of the runway's centerline as a reference to track. 5. A climbing turn to the left, initiated at an altitude four hundred feet above the runway, onto the cross wind leg of the pattern. 6. A level-out at pattern altitude; eight hundred feet above the runway. 7. A turn to the left onto the downwind leg of the pattern. 8. The downwind leg, parallel to the runway but in the direction opposite a landing. 9. The reduction of power to begin the approach. 10. An extension of the downwind leg during the first stage of descent in the approach. 11. A descending turn to the left onto the base leg of the pattern. 12. Continued descent along the base leg. 13. A descending turn to the left onto the final leg of the pattern; 14. The final approach, flown in alignment with the imaginary extension of the runway's centerline; 15. The flare out. 16. Touch down. 17; Roll out. 18. An exit from the active runway, preparatory to taxiing back to start it all again.

To use an airport backwards means that people are landing downwind.

To land down T means to land contrary to the indications of a wind T; to go down a one-way street the wrong way.

Touch and go refers to a landing that is complete through all phases of the approach, including touch down, but then is interrupted in the roll-out by taking off again.

To make a straight-in approach means to proceed directly to the final leg of the approach without first flying a conventional pattern.

To go on around or fly a missed approach means to abandon an approach at any point in the landing pattern, though usually on the final leg before the flare out, and then to add power and climb back up to pattern altitude again, from there to re-enter the pattern and fly a new approach.

To crank in trim relieves the pilot from holding constant back-pressure and is especially helpful during an approach in holding an airspeed. The trim is a mechanical system beginning with a trim wheel located in the cockpit and leading to a trim tab or other appendage located on the elevators of the airplane. Cranking in trim produces a nose-up rotation of the airplane.

To crab is to compensate for a cross wind by heading the airplane slightly into the wind. A <u>crab angle</u> is the common name for such an angle. <u>Wind correction angle</u> is the technical name.

<u>To true the wheels with the direction of travel</u> insures that the wheels touch down true to the direction the airplane is moving. Failure to do this leads to sidling, bouncing, and a tendency to veer.

<u>To hold a slip during the flare</u> means to continue side-slipping into the wind to correct for drift in a cross wind landing. The ailerons roll the airplane <u>into</u> the wind, thus producing a turn whose turn-radius is equal to and opposite the lateral drift. At the same time, the rudder yaws the airplane <u>with</u> the wind, thus maintaining the wheels true to the direction of travel.

A <u>one-wheel landing</u> is the result of landing in a slip.

<u>To get behind in an approach</u> connotes a failure by the pilot to keep up with developments, especially as they pertain to compensating for wind and correcting for misjudgments and errors.

<u>To keep ahead in an approach</u> implies the opposite, in which the pilot has anticipated what will happen and what might.

<u>To grease it on</u> means to land an airplane so subtly that it is the sound of the tires rolling and not the feel of contact with the ground that tells the pilot the airplane is down.

<u>To cream it on</u> describes a landing so smooth that it ends up that evening as news.

www.ingramcontent.com/pod-product-compliance
Lightning Source LLC
Chambersburg PA
CBHW070605100426
42744CB00006B/403